MW01491622

, 2021 6:54:58 PM***null-3501S485-KNZ968YC-214

Lions of Marjah

Combat as I Saw It

By Ryan N. Rogers
SGT. USMC

RYAN N. ROGERS

Lions of Marjah –

Combat as I Saw It

ISBN 978-0-578-89122-4

Copyright © 2021 by Ryan N. Rogers

All rights reserved. No part of this publication can be reproduced or transmitted, including by electron means without prior written permission from the publisher. For permission requests, email the publisher at Rogersryan063@gmail.com. All events, places, names, and actions are my personal experiences and my interpretation and best recollection of them. Copyright drives creativity and authentic thought. Language is the verbal form of thinking and writing the extension of thought to benefit others. Thank you for buying a copy of this book and for abiding by all copyright laws. This supports authentic writing and authors everywhere.

Front and back cover images by Tyler Hicks.

Book design by Donna Lynn.

Edited by Debbie Burke.

Author photo (c) Ian Fowler Photography.

LIONS OF MARJAH

null-35015485-KNZ968YC-214

RYAN N. ROGERS

Dedication

This book is dedicated to Matthias Hanson, Erick Currier, Joey Harms, The Squad, and my entire family/friend support network that urged me to finish.

This book was written for the warfighter from the very beginning, from the notes made in the dim night from a mud hut to the completed version today. I have made my best attempt to remain apolitical and keep the scope of information oriented to my combat experience.

"Good people do what they find honorable to do, even if it requires hard work; they'll even do it if it causes them injury; they'll even do it if it will bring danger. Again, they won't do what they find base, even if it brings wealth, pleasure, or power. Nothing will deter them from what is honorable, and nothing will lure them into what is base."

- Seneca, Moral Letters, 76.18

LIONS OF MARJAH

LIONS OF MARJAH

Orders

After being in the Marines for just over 2 ½ years of my five-year contract I had seen a lot and been in a couple of different units. I started out in the FAST (fleet anti-terrorism security team) company out of Norfolk, VA, where I did a Cuba fence line deployment and a deployment to Bahrain where my platoon was a quick reaction force for the Southeast Asia's US embassies.

Following my bid in FAST Company I received orders to 3rd Battalion 2nd Marines out of Camp Lejeune, North Carolina. At this point my composite score was just short of picking up Corporal. In the Corps we have a scoring system that virtually grades us. They take your physical fitness scores, your proficiency and conduct marks, your rifle range score and some other items and average out a score. Then you compete for promotion. When your score meets or exceeds the minimum promotion score, you are promoted. Something to know about Security Force Marines is this: Fleet Marines do not like us; for good reason, too. They graduated the School Of Infantry SOI and went straight to the operating forces and deployed to combat one or two times in their first two years. We graduated SOI and went to another school followed by two years in a unit that typically did not deploy into a combat zone, and a lot of the time would check into the operating forces not knowing shit about the infantry. Even worse, we would be corporals taking over teams or squads that "seasoned Lance Corporals" felt that they deserved.

As a LCpl. in Lima Company 3/2 I was put in the squad leader billet for the first time in my short career. A few months of training later, I pinned on another stripe. All the time in the Corps to that point I had still seen no combat. I had waited so long and with Iraq slowing down, I was thankful for a squad but starting to think my chances of seeing combat were slimming down, like a Viking missing the raiding tour.

Later that year, I deployed as a squad leader to Al Quim, Iraq, near the Syrian border. Here I spent a lot of time in BP Tarawa in a town called Karbala. I also spent a short period of time at Camp Gannon and the end of my pump on or near COP Rahwa; all generally in the same area.

I spent seven months in Iraq to see a minimum amount of combat. I did get a ton of experience out patrolling the streets every day in both urban, built-up areas and rural wide-open farm towns. At the least, I became better as a squad leader, but I got into zero firefights. The most was a few separate occasions where we received pop shots, and three occasions where we had IEDs go off in our convoy or on the ground near us. It just wasn't as kinetic as I thought or wished it would be. Had I known then what I know now, I would have been perfectly fine with that.

Shortly after returning from Iraq, I found out that our next deployment was going to be on the 24th Marine Expeditionary Unit MEU, and I was coming up on my EAS (End of Active Service) date. I had about 12 months to decide what I wanted to do about staying in or getting out. Quickly I decided if I did stay in the Corps, I didn't want to stay with 3/2, so I tried out for the All Marine Boxing team. It was a situation where if I got on the team, I would go TAD (Temporary Assignment of Duty) to the boxing team from 3/2. I figured it would at least buy me some time before re-upping. I got on the team and remained there for just over nine months. After nine months and a five and one record, it was time to go back to 3/2, that was now on the 24th MEU. I would either get out of the Corps or reenlist and get new orders. I took the latter option, hanging on still to the dream and thirst for combat. With Iraq drawing completely down at this point and Afghanistan on the verge of heating back up again, I went to the career planner and told him I wanted the first deploying unit to Afghanistan. That went nowhere, as he began to tell me how hard it is just to jump into the next unit pushing out; everyone was doing the same thing in my MOS. I made it perfectly clear that I wanted a combat deployment and I let him work on it for a While A few weeks later I was called in and told that I had to decide, re-up or move on in life. I once again went with the re-up. I reenlisted in the Marines to stay with the second Marine Regiment on an Operational forces incentive package. I would remain with 3/2 until Regimental Combat Team 2 was stood up

RYAN N. ROGERS

for Afghanistan. When the regiment stood up, I would be a squad leader in Colonel Kennedy's PSD (Private Security Detail). I was pumped. While in the transition process, I became good friends with Steve Herbst ("Herby"), Scott Davis ("Scotty D") and Tim Smith ("Timbo"). By that I mean we drank a lot and blamed it on 8th Comm…. We hung out a good bit every day and stayed tight until a decision was made.

After two weeks I was called by my career planner and told I had orders to 3rd Battalion 6th Marines.

I was infuriated because 3/6 was scheduled to go to Okinawa for seven months to train. I bitched like Marines bitch and got nowhere other than 3/6. The only thing I had going for me was that I had a few guys I knew pretty well from 3/2 going with me. We all checked in on September 17th, 2009. Upon checking in we fell under Headquarters Company, as the Sergeant Major had not met us due to leave. Therefore, we weren't assigned to a certain company. We mainly did little odds and ends around the company or went home early and stayed low-key.

Once the Sergeant Major came back off leave, the guys and I all reported in to him and he assigned us each to our companies. Herby and I were assigned to Kilo Company. Assigned to Kilo Company as well were friends Scott Davis and Tim Smith. The others we came with were Paul Williams ("Pauly") and Billy Boone ("Bill Bill") who were assigned to Headquarters Company.

We were set to check in to our Company 1st Sgt and Company Commander the following day by 0800. So we all went home for the day and prepared our uniforms for the following morning.

I'll start off by saying that being late the day you are supposed to check in to your new company is just a little bit stupid. Waiting on Herby that day was a mistake. That mistake got me introduced to Gunnery Sergeant McCarver, the kind of gunny who just looks like he's a solid 10 years older than you know he is. He has that sun-tanned, leathery skin with the smell of cigarettes on his clothes and some Copenhagen snuff fine cut packed in his lip, glaring with his eyes squinted, displaying Clint

Eastwood-style crow's feet in the outside corners of his eyes. Starting your bid in a new company by making "that" company gunny chew your ass so bad he nearly has a nosebleed and spits three quarters of his dip out in the process is a mistake. After a nice 30-minute ass-chewing about how "on time is late and early is on time" the smoke cleared out of his ears and 1st Sergeant Petrakos greeted us. Though he was not happy we were late, he remained somewhat civil compared to the company gunny. We talked for a while, mostly about how the company ran and his expectations for us within the company, and then he sent us to get some chow. He told us to be back at 1300 and he would assign us to our platoons.

We were on time for our 1300 meeting by being there at 1245 like studious little Marines, at which point 1st Sergeant Petrakos assigned Herby who was the only one with a weapons MOS to weapons platoon (he was an 0331 Machine Gunner). The rest of us being 0311 rifleman went to rifle platoons. Scott Davis and I both went to 2nd Platoon and Tim Smith to 1st Platoon. At this point we were all corporals, though I was right on the Sergeant cutting score due to pick up the next quarter. I was excited to finally be dropping to a company. Once dropped to the company I would be able to begin observing the Marines I would be working with and how proficient the company was both technically and tactically.

When I went to meet my platoon sergeant, I was told he was going through Small Unit Leaders Course and was "out of pocket" as he had been in a car accident the week prior. The first person I met from the platoon was Sgt. Creel. He was, at the time, the platoon's Second Squad leader. He told me that our Platoon Commander 1st Lt. Emmanuel was also "out of pocket," as he was at Mountain Leaders Course. I was given my initial counseling and taken over to the barracks to meet the platoon. As I always did when joining a new unit, I introduced myself and then hung back and mostly observed how the platoon operated for a few days. Just as you would in every other job, I observed and tried to read the Marines before jumping right in under some false pretense that they would just accept me with open arms.

You see, that's just not the way that Marines are built. They are built to be hard, especially to those who they don't know anything about. And let's be honest; no one likes a new guy coming in to try and take over your situation.

At this point, having not met the platoon sergeant and or the platoon commander, I really had no billet within the platoon. I was just going off hearsay from the other Marines about where I would be put and who was staying for the pump and who wasn't. I had heard that the 3rd Squad Leader Sgt. Kelk was coming up on his EAS and he was planning to get out. I heard that Sgt. Creel was unsure but most likely staying for the pump, and that the 1st Squad Leader Sgt. Hind was 100% sure he was staying. Once again, at this point, we were slated for an Okinawa deployment. I had high hopes of taking a squad from either of the sergeants who might leave the platoon for EAS, as I had come from 3/2 as a squad leader. I sure didn't want to go backwards, not to mention I was going to be a sergeant in less than 30 days.

Two weeks after joining the platoon, my composite score was where it needed to be, and it was time for me to get promoted and claim my third stipe and rightful place in the platoon. I still hadn't met my platoon sergeant or platoon commander.

I was promoted on the 7th of November because the company was busy training. We started that week with a terrifying training event where you are in a simulated helicopter crash underwater. We had to conduct this training since we were Helicopter Company. Basically, you go to a building with a big pool in it and receive several hours of classes on ditching birds over water and how to survive. Day two, you get in the pool where instructors try to get you nice and comfortable by doing some drills with you. They would have us put our legs up on the side of the pool and then push us under until we were straight down, back flat, on the pool wall, under water. Then you clear and breathe with a can of air (breathing apparatus). After that you sit in these little chairs that simulate being a passenger in a bird all buckled in, and they flip you upside down into the water, at which point you go through the seat belt removal procedures and get out of the chair. Not so bad.

That's just the start.

Day three starts with the Helo (helicopter) dunker. It's like a hollowed-out Helo simulator that you buckle into and then they drop it from six or eight feet over the water and into the water you go. But it's on hydraulics, and when you hit the water it rotates you under each way left and right. Meaning, when you're buckled in, you're either going to rotate forward and take a breath going face first into the water, or you're going straight down and back into the water. If you don't know which way you're going in, it can get tricky. You have less time when going backwards to get your breath.

The morning of day three prior to going to the pool for all that fun stuff I was promoted. They had a nice formation for me and everything. When I center marched to report into the commanding officer to have my promotion warrant read, I had my new chevrons in my right hand. When a Marine gets promoted in front of a formation, he marches on command and salutes the officer he is reporting to. With my sergeant chevrons in my right hand, my salute was all dicked up. I lost all composure and gripped the chevrons with my pinky and ring finger and gave my new commanding officer a two-finger head nod salute. He kind of frowned at me as if to say "Really motherfucker?" then went about pinning me. What a horrible first impression. My CO at the time was Captain J. P. Biggers. An extremely in-shape prior Recon Marine, who later became a man I will always respect. He didn't do what he could have done and blow me up on the spot for being stupid. He just gave me a look of "what the fuck" and never mentioned it again.

- Early is on time, on time is late.

RYAN N. ROGERS

22 MILES

In the second week of November, just after the Helo dunker, was a 20-mile conditioning hike. From what I gathered, once again from the Marines second-hand, they had hiked like every other week starting at three miles working up to 15 miles before I came to the company. The last time I had put any kind of weight on my back and grunted it out on a hike was when I was in 3/2 prior to deploying to Iraq, which at this point was a year and some change in the past. There were rumors floating around that Davis and I were going to get put on duty as to not look like ball bags in front of the junior Marines, if in fact we fell back or out of the hike. This was honestly a pretty wise decision made by the command knowing that we didn't work up to that kind of distance with the company. Davis had at least one of the duties on hike day locked because he had recently had surgery on his wrist. I was to take the other one; but I didn't take it. Not because I love to hike, by any means; simply because these Marines don't know me from Adam, and if I never give them a reason to start to trust me or at least establish some sort of dominance, it will suck for me and for them when I take a squad.

We started the hike around 2200 that Thursday night, with full combat gear and about 50-pound packs, packing out M240 along with their "A" bags and tripods. I led Second Squad during the hike. To get the Marines to see I was not half bad I carried the 240 for the last four out of six legs of the hike. I will have you know I was broke the fuck off. We took "River PT Road "on Lejeune out to the tank trails and then back. Somewhere during our tank trail portion someone made a wrong turn either accidentally or intentionally; I don't know, but it added two miles to the hike. I remember being 100% done on the way back with the 240 whipping my ass and seeing the lights to the softball field in the distance. That was our stopping point. It was sometime around six in the morning.

Finally, after six hours and some change, the front of the formation made a right down into the softball field and wheeled around it in a square until all companies were down and we came

LIONS OF MARJAH

to a halt. I couldn't have been happier. Then I heard the sergeant major call up the company 1st sergeants and tell them to get their "tug of war" teams ready from each company. I had no clue what was going on. I had never even done a hike that long, let alone been forced to play tug of war at the end of it. I just so happened to be selected for the company's team! Given the fact that everyone in the company was completely spent anyway, we gave a valiant effort and lost. The hike concluded with Lt. Colonel Christmas giving a motivational speech about not just getting to the fight but having enough left when you get to the fight, to win the fight. At this point the entire company was starting to cramp up and just wanted a shower and to conduct some rack ops.

We were released to our platoon sergeants and sent to the barracks to shower and go to bed, as they wouldn't let anyone who lived out in town drive until they had a minimum of five hours of sleep. We made our way back to the barracks mostly talking about how we were going to go get some Subway and go to bed. In the shower I came to realize that the entire bottom of both of my feet were gone. It was one big blister that popped and peeled off during the hike. So instead of going to Subway, I slept doubled up on a rack with a kid from Second Squad named Michael Grimes until 1200 when we were released for the weekend.

The following week was when I had heard that my platoon sergeant was going to be back. I was starting to get to know the Marines and I was ready to meet the boss. With the day drawing to a close, the platoon was called out to the rifle wash racks in the quad to get the word. As we fell out and moved into the quad, I saw a behemoth of a man standing tall and half-slouched over at the same time burning a Marlboro Red, awaiting the platoon. Once the platoon was gathered around the staff sergeant for the word, he began by lighting up another smoke. He got about two or three minutes into the brief when he snapped over, locked eyes with me and said, "Who the fuck are you?" I replied with my name and told him I was a new addition to the platoon coming from 3/2. He said, "Very well." And the meeting was over. After the word was passed, I met back up with staff sergeant and

RYAN N. ROGERS

received his expectations brief, and was then introduced to my platoon commander.

When I first met the lieutenant, I was a bit skeptical, to say the least. He was a black man who stood about 5 foot 10, pretty in shape athletic build, with a damn-near shaved head. I started out skeptical because to that point in my career I had never met a platoon commander that was worth his weight. The thing that I did like, however, was that he gave me his expectations right up front and was very direct, very blunt.

At that point in time, I would have never guessed that he would become the person who, next to my own mother and father, I would come to respect more than any person, and ultimately the one Marine in my career whom I would always try to emulate.

The next day was a platoon commanders' PT session. One thing that was not mentioned the day before during my expectations brief from LT was the fact that he was really fast and very in shape. The three-and-some-change mile run he took the platoon on was miserable, to say the least. I loved the fact that my platoon commander was so involved with the platoon, and the fact that he was so in shape. This did two things for me: made me strive to be better and seek self-improvement; and made me gain respect and confidence in my leadership. Funny how just a short run can do so much more for a unit than just condition them.

I can say this as well, the staff sergeant and lieutenant worked great as a team. They jived off one another very well. They were always together on every decision, at least in the platoon's eyes, and that was what mattered. One unified front, a Unity of Command. They would always be together observing training if not participating. Even during the smallest little evolutions such as practicing on and offs with tourniquets, they were always there.

- To the Marines reading this, you will find that a unified front on the small unit level works tremendously better than the alternative. Find it, foster it.

RYAN N. ROGERS

President Barack Obama Approves a Significant Troop Increase for Afghanistan

On December 2nd, 2009 President Barak Obama ordered an extra 30,000 troops to deploy to Afghanistan in support of Operation Enduring Freedom. This was not a decision the president took lightly at all. Upon the initial request from General Stanley McChrystal, the president reportedly deliberated on whether to sign off on the surge for nearly three months. Gen Stanley McChrystal, the US commander in Afghanistan, welcomed the speech, saying he had been given "a clear military mission" and the necessary resources.

As you might imagine, this was amazing news for the lot of us. At this point 3/6 was about one month out from deploying, making us one of the most-ready combat elements in the chute. With the battalion only a few short months and the company only six weeks, I was still super pumped at the slightest chance that we would get called off the Oki deployment and sent to Afghanistan. I was starting to get a good feel for the platoon now and was completely turned over as the Second Squad leader.

I can't tell you the emotions the week leading up to the decision from the Marine Corps to put us on this mission; I just know that when the word was finalized and we were going over to Afghanistan instead of Okinawa I was elated. Maybe I wouldn't miss combat after all.

Just before pushing out on pre-deployment leave there were rumors spreading about a Taliban stronghold in a city called Marjah, somewhere in the Helmand River Valley Province. The rumors were that there would be an assault on the stronghold involving elements from 1/6 and 3/6. We soon found out that they were not rumors.

Now with my company for just under two months, I had started to get to know my squad. I hadn't memorized all their names, but I was close. Second Squad was not the ideal squad that you would ask for on the dawn of the hardest fight of your life. What they would become, however, is a different story altogether. The team leaders were Cpl. Jesse Bennett, Cpl. Matthew Charette, and Cpl. John Simmering. Bennett was my number one, a solid-ass Marine, one whom I would trust my squad to in case I was taken out of the fight. He was a knowledgeable Marine who had great work ethic and personal drive. He was an avid hunter like me and from Ohio like me. He also came up in the Marine Corps in FAST Company, stationed in Norfolk, VA like myself. So, like me in many ways, we initially bumped heads. We were both alpha males and he had a chip on his shoulder because he was in line to take the squad leader position until I arrived on deck. All that said, he was a great leader. To be honest, I love that in a Marine. I would rather have three team leaders who fight to take my job and want my job than three who are less confident and aggressive. If they fight for my job it means they are probably as good or better in their eyes and it forces me to keep my shit quick, and ultimately the squad is better for it.

Cpl. Matthew Charette hailed from the not-so-great state of Massachusetts. Matt's dad was a corrections officer and his mother was the police chief of the small town where he grew up. Sorry bastard must have had it rough as hell growing up. Mr. and Mrs. Charette raised a damn good man, though. He was a good Marine who had unlimited potential. Matt wasn't sure about me at first, but we would grow to become great friends. He was somewhat secluded at first, kind of feeling me out as a leader. He had felt betrayed by Sgt. Creel who, upon getting the information that we were deploying to Marjah, decided to go a different direction. The thing about Matt, though, was that I could say *get something done* and with zero supervision he would get said mission accomplished. "Jerry-rigged" or not, that's an amazing attribute in a Marine.

Cpl. Simmering was my number three. He had come from First Battalion First Marines, where I had several buddies. Knowing this I called my best friend Matt Burke, formally from 1-1, inquiring about Simmering. I found that he was not a team leader over there but did have some combat experience. Though he had experience I was informed that he was a Marine to keep a watchful eye on due to performance. I heeded advice and cautiously made him my third TL.

The rest of the squad consisted of several great Marines; all boots, however. In first team you had LCpl. Maciewicz on the M-203/M4. Mac could touch you with HEDP (high explosive dual purpose) anywhere inside of 350 yards. He was surgical with that thing. LCpl. Knuckles on the M-249 squad automatic weapon (SAW) was an amazing Marine who was being groomed to take a team the following deployment. Cpl. Bennett, who was the 1st team leader/designated marksman carrying a MK12, made up 1st team. LCpl. Sullivan was formally with this team but was pulled to be a dog handler and hadn't returned yet. Second team, under Cpl. Charette, was LCpl. Wetzel who ran point for the team and ultimately the squad; PFC Bridges whom I received from the School of Infantry two days into pre-deployment leave; and LCpl. Wright aka Minime, a nickname he received from our platoon sergeant, Staff Sergeant Wright. The difference was that SSgt. Wright was a 6'2" large white man and Minime was a 5'5" tiny little black man. It was a running joke with the platoon. Bridges was on the SAW. Cpl. Charette carried the M-203/M4. Team Three was made up by Cpl. Simmering carrying an M16, LCpl. Grimes carried a M4-203 and Vuocolo (V) was the team's SAW gunner.

Going Away

Going home to Ohio was a bittersweet time, as it always is for pre-deployment leave. The family is always on edge and you, as the Marine leaving, always feel obligated to try to make everyone feel better about it. I had a good time visiting with everyone until the last night. I started to get into the conversation with my dad about deploying. I told him that this one was going to be rough and that he should probably not watch too much of the coverage on TV if there was any. That conversation was very long and emotional, ending with him telling me with tears in his eyes to always think about the situation and to do what he knew I could. I remember him saying over and over, "Son, you can do everything right in this game and still people get killed. Don't increase the odds by rushing into a bad spot. Always measure twice and cut once." It was the carpenter's rule he would always bring up. I also remember him using bow hunting large whitetail bucks as an example. "The buck didn't get to be so big by being stupid; he got so big because he was never complacent. You must outsmart him with you mind. Whenever he got a gut feeling or his baseline environment changed, he bailed out the same way he came in." The conversation ended late that evening.

Returning to North Carolina was almost a relief, though now I had to face the hardest goodbye yet. The last night was a very emotional one for my wife. This was her first deployment as well, not making it any easier. The night ended with us making love and then me holding her as she cried for hours, softly and quietly, as I held her until she fell asleep. For me, all I could think about was bringing my Marines back home in seven months. For the sake of not making her any more upset, I left that comment out of the equation.

Every Marine has a different way of going about saying goodbye the day they leave. Some invite their whole family, some none at all. Some get emotional, some not at all. Some Marines sleep, some are wired to the teeth with excitement. For me, though, I have my wife there for the first couple of hours, but

RYAN N. ROGERS

as the time draws near to boarding the buses, I ask her to leave. There are already enough emotions to deal with just in the squad; I don't need my own clouding the air. As soon as she is out of sight, I flip the switch in my head and become a different person altogether. The me I become is 100% focused on the mission at hand.

This farewell caught me off guard a bit. I was rounding up the boys and I got a stern grab on the shoulder. It was Vuocolo's father, a two-tour Vietnam veteran. He looked me in the eyes stone cold and said, "Bring 'em all home, one way or another you bring these boys home." I swallowed hard, trying to not look shaken as tears welled up in my eyes and started to roll down my cheeks. The bitter January chill made it feel like tiny paths of ice and emotion were visible to all who were present. "Yes Sir, you have my word on that." He then turned to his son and just when Travis leaned in to hug his father possibly for the last time, his Dad put his hand out, stopped him and they shook. "Kill 'em good," his dad said, with tears in his eyes. It was definitely an emotional exchange of words between father and son, and between father and the son's leader in combat. Many times, throughout the course of the deployment, these words were all but drilling into my forebrain to stay in the present. Stay humble, measure twice/cut once, bring them all home.

We boarded the bus and away we went, off to Cherry Point. The ride was quiet as it always is on the way off base. By about 20 minutes into it, though, the Marines all began to loosen up and converse. Marines, in my experience, tend to talk more when they are nervous. Coming into this deployment, I am certain that most everyone was a bit concerned. I know, at least for myself, this had the potential to be the biggest fight of my life. Once at Cherry Point, we did the customary rigamarole and awaited our flight.

Let me define a bit what I mean when I say "awaited our flight." It starts with already being excited and having that adrenaline pump; in turn, everyone is chatty as hell and wants to have fun. So, several decks of cards get broken out and the endless games of spades commence. After several hours of this the Marines begin to lose the "we are deploying today" high and start to get sleepy. This stage of waiting can be very fun or not very fun at all. For Marines like me, it is fun because when everyone starts falling asleep, it's shenanigan time. For Marines that fall asleep it becomes get fucked with time. I am not sure how many bootlaces were tied together or to other bootlaces, but it was a lot. While at Cherry Point during the wind-down phase we received word that we would be staying the night and flying out first thing in the morning. One word comes to mind: "Fuck!" The next morning, we boarded the flight and left American soil for possibly the last time.

The flight over is long and horrible; let's just call it what it is. It takes like 18 to 22 hours depending on where your stops are and how long you lay over at each place. Sometimes it's Shannon, Ireland, for an hour and sometimes it's Ramstein, Germany, for four. But that's not the bad part. The bad part is while in flight. Yeah, they show movies and have music to listen to but after your third movie you are over it. Many Marines like to take a bit of Nyquil to aid them in a nice little slumber and some are prescribed meds like Ambien to do the trick. Either way you try to get as much sleep as possible. It keeps you from being tired on top of having jet lag and makes the trip go by much faster. The plane ride is much like the bus ride in terms of the Marines' chattiness. They are all chatty initially but then the "what ifs" begin to mount, and for some, they are just realizing the gravity of the situation. Unfortunately, it's a fact that the Corps will teach you everything about killing, and everything about being the best and never being afraid; stating that these attributes are those of weak people and they will cause hesitation on the field of battle. The issue there becomes that most of that is bullshit. In country, being afraid keeps you vigilant and vigilance keeps you alive. Not being afraid will allow complacency in and complacency kills. You can see this in every country on every gate of a US base for a reason. I remember one junior Marine who thought he was the "cock of the walk" when it came to be ready to kill and ready to go, but he also was the one throwing up on the plane because he hadn't accepted what he was embarking on. One thing is for sure, the flight into war is the wrong time to start questioning anything. I can only imagine what some of the super young Marines like Bridges or Breland were thinking. They had been out of the School of Infantry for fewer than 60 days.

Getting into country is not just some direct commercial flight, as you probably already know. It's an ass bleed of customs and connections. We stopped on the way over in Germany to refuel and then ultimately ended our commercial trip at Manas Air Base in Kyrgyzstan. Kyrgyzstan is a small country that borders Afghanistan to the north. We landed there and stayed a few nights waiting for our not-so-commercial military lift into Afghanistan. Only being there for a few days, we spent our time packing day packs and palletizing our big gear. One evening while the whole company was out palletizing gear, it was freezing cold and started to snow. The company 1st sergeant was a stickler on keeping your hands out of your pockets, as well as uniformity throughout the company. Simply put, we all had to wear the same thing. If one Marine was wearing a soft cover, we all wore a soft cover; if one was wearing a fleece jacket, we all wore a fleece jacket, and so on. It was so cold this night that we all started to stand in a warming circle while waiting for more gear to pack. In short, a warming circle is a very sketchy, semi mosh-pit with no music, everyone butt to nut trying to siphon warmth off all he was in contact with. The boots were always on the outside for some reason. First sergeant walked up with his hands in his pockets, a beanie on his head and a shit-eating grin on his face and said, "Damn Marines are yaw stupid. It's cold as shit out here, use the pockets and dress warmer." This got a pretty good chuckle out of the whole company, immediately followed by warming layers coming out of the woodwork. Beanies were going on heads, sweatshirts were coming from somewhere I don't even know at this point, and from afar it must have looked like a bait ball erupting to the surface of the intercoastal as a school of red drum drives them. We all as a company arrived in Kyrgyzstan on the same evening but we would be leaving on C130s in multiple sticks (groups on a flight).

LIONS OF MARJAH

So finally, after about a million games of spades again with the boys, it was time to board. Our next stop would be Camp Leatherneck in Afghanistan. Camp Leatherneck was a 1600-acre Marine Corps base located in Helmand Province. It was initially developed in 2008 when the troop count in country was still on the rise. It is in the Washir District and partnered up with Camp Bastion, which is the main British base in Afghanistan.

Camp Leatherneck was a staging area for our assault into Marjah. We landed and did the typical Marine Corps shuffle to get all our gear squared away and get to our berthing. Only being just south of Kyrgyzstan it was still quite cold. Once we were on deck for a day or so, we had a schedule of things to accomplish. The "every deployment" things like ROE (rules of engagement) briefs from the battalion adjutant and last-minute administrative paperwork. We also conducted daily PT and even a live fire range to confirm our battle zeros for our personal rifles. After a couple of weeks at Leatherneck we received orders that the company would be again taking flight and would be landing at a small FOB (Forward Operating Position) called Camp Dwyer.

Camp Dwyer was in the Helmand River Valley, in the Garmsir District. It was and still is a US Marine airfield. The airfield was named after British Lance Bombardier James Dwyer of the 29th Commando Regiment, Royal Artillery. He was killed in action in December of 2006 in Helmand Province.

We would stay and train at Camp Dwyer until it was time to execute, which to this point we did not know. We again went through a daily PT regiment and trained on the squad level for everything we could think of. We practiced putting tourniquets on one another, we cleaned weapons, we practiced our communications with all radios we had, I even sought out an artillery officer and got classes from him on how to call for different types of ordnance; things like HIMAR rockets and Excalibur artillery rounds that were completely new to me and somewhat new to the Marine Corps. Camp Dwyer is also where we would receive our Afghan Army counterparts that would be pushing with us.

RYAN N. ROGERS

ANA (Afghanistan National Army) soldiers were issued to us almost like a piece of gear. A squad of ANA would be attached to a squad of Marines and so on. I will start by saying we are two totally different cultures. You hear that and think "yeah clearly," but you don't really understand it until you are living day in and day out with someone from another culture, especially when they have never even seen a bathroom or a toilet before. They have only ever shit and pissed in the canals or in a small hole they dig in the sand floors of their homes. We had to teach them everything. On the first evening upon bringing them into our berthing, it was late, and I needed to shower. I made my way to the shower tent under the light of my headlamp, I was in my flip-flops and green silkies with my shower bag and towel in hand. The shower tent had a heavy flap for a door to block out the light and obviously for privacy. I threw open the flap and entered the shower tent. It was the foulest smell maybe that I had ever smelled before. The ANA, never having amenities like these in their entire lives, didn't understand how to use them. They had piles and piles of feces on top of the toilets, on top the toilet seats, all over the floor; and as if that wasn't bad enough, they turned to the sinks. I left instantly only being in the tent for a few seconds, and still woke up the next morning with conjunctivitis. Doc gave me some strong eye cream to clear it up fast, but it was still a big slap in the face as to the cultural divide.

This is where training paid dividends. Knowing that my guys were locked on gave me some freedom to focus on training the ANA. Having to train an adult to use the shitter is less fun than training your child.

- Beware of what you wish for. Know the culture that you're stepping into, and always train...like your life may depend on it.

The Attack Order

After a few weeks in country we were moved from Leatherneck to Camp Dwyer and we were getting a bit restless. We trained every day. We practiced putting tourniquets on one another and loading frequencies into the radios. I ensured that my team leaders and I worked every day on properly calling every fire mission from mortars to HIMARS as well as calling in a CASEVAC 9 line. We even set up a makeshift range outside the wire in the desert and conducted a live-fire attack complete with an APOBS (anti-personnel obstacle breaching system) shot, machine guns, and RPG fire. That range was the first and only time we worked integrated with our Afghan soldier counterparts prior to the fight in Marjah. It was great to fire the weapons but even better to work with our ANA and build the trust and confidence in each other.

With tensions running high you could just feel it in the air that everyone was ready to go; that feeling of anxiousness that you have all day Friday at school knowing that at 7 p.m. that night you would be playing in the biggest football game of your life. Or the way you feel on a perfect morning in the tree stand when you know that today will be the day that you take a shot on a massive whitetail. For the junior level guys, the experience of deploying was all brand new and therefore I know it was nerve-wracking from the beginning. The experienced Marines remained cool and collected much more easily, but very few from our company had ever been part of an operation of this magnitude. That being the case, the leadership was all a bit giddy as well. The mood started to get a bit more intense when the command came out and told us the phones were about to be shut down and that the date would soon be upon us. That could only mean that the Operation Order was coming and that they didn't want to have some dumbass Marine calling home and telling Suzie all about the mission, completely blowing our operational security (OPSEC).

I didn't know it then, but Captain Biggers, our company commander, had already briefed the company order to the lieutenants and select key personnel of the company. He gave

RYAN N. ROGERS

them the broad brush strokes on the bigger picture. For the regular general population (GP) Marine rifleman, it's what we call the big blue arrow. Letting platoons know what their mission is and attaching supporting arms, that kind of thing. Platoon sergeants and platoon commanders found out where everyone would be and who was adjacent to whom; and key terrain features and Areas of Interest (AOL), as well as the tentative company scheme of maneuver. All on a higher level, on the company level. It was given, I assume, in much the same way LT gave our platoon order, via PowerPoint presentation. This enables the use of pictures of objectives and a more detailed briefing.

See, it works like this. The battalion commander gives his order to the company commanders, and they take from his order certain details and instructions but most importantly his commander's intent. What he wants as an end state, what will be done at the end of the day! The company commanders compile all this information and build their own company order to give to their platoon commanders. In turn, the lieutenants build the platoon order to brief to the platoons.

When it was time to get the order, the entire platoon was herded into a big troop tent on Dwyer directly across from the tent that we all were staying in. As I entered the tent behind my squad, I could feel my blood pressure going up. I knew it was time. Time to get some answers: who, what, when, where and why; what exactly my mission was and the sequence of events that would ensue. LT started out with a nicely put-together PowerPoint five-paragraph order much like the captain gave. He covered everything to a T and left no questions unanswered. Once the order was over, LT turned off the PowerPoint and got really serious really quick. He started by saying "Fuck these motherfuckers" then went on about a 30-minute talk about how not to freeze or hesitate, and how we all came here together and that's how we're going to leave. He started to even get a bit emotional through some of it. To this point in the deployment, it was the first time I was inspired by someone in my command through language. Ironically, he ended the speech by asking everyone to bow our heads, and regardless of color or creed we all bowed. He asked God to watch over us and concluded with "Amen" after a few more short words. After the prayer we all broke and headed back to the berthing to get ready.

We would be moving back to Camp Leatherneck in the following days, where we would launch our assault. The order lieutenant gave what would always be known afterward, to the Marines of Kilo Company 2nd Platoon, as the "Fuck These Motherfuckers" speech. I earnestly believe he was trying to capture everyone's attention and really institute the gravity of the mission we were now about to embark on. The speech was geared toward the enemy only, in almost a respectful manner; as in, don't think about his feelings or yours, 'because he's not going to give you that same privilege. Be better, be faster, communicate, execute. The leadership shown by a man of only 24 or 25 years old in a freezing cold desert when he himself must have been terrified was impeccable. The fire and passion in his eyes led to inspiration amongst us all. Some say leaders can be built and others say that leaders are born. I believe leaders are born and emerge when the conditions are necessary for such an emergence. Where that comes from, I don't know.

One funny thing about Infantry Marines; no matter what unit they are in or came from, we all tend to deal with stress and death the same way. We cope nine times out of 10 by humor. We make fun of and laugh about things that would make a common person cry and or puke. For instance, right after the LT's order we all went back to our berthing and getting the raw facts that we were about to be in the biggest fight of our life, everyone was stressed to the max and filled with nervous emotion. The Marines didn't let me down, though. As I cleaned my weapon on my rack and talked with JT and Hinde (the other two squad leaders in the platoon) about the upcoming day's events, a 2nd Platoon Marine began to blast Taylor Swift's latest album through an iHome. Before I knew it, there were Marines singing every word in unison and even some running through the hooch stripping and dancing. Everyone laughed hysterically, and the nerves were somewhat suppressed. One thing you can always count on with a group of grunts is humor from horror. You will have your ones and twos that you need to keep an eye on and, as a mentor, talk to. Sometimes the emotions and thoughts of dying will come up. But in the infantry community in my experience, these Marines are very few and far between.

A few short days following the company receiving our order we packed and palletized all gear once more and took flight back to Camp Leatherneck to stage for the invasion of Marjah.

The morning of February 12th we were set to roll and started to pack the buses to make our way to the other side of the base where the LZ (landing zone) was located. It was dark and we were crammed in buses with all our shit we would be inserting with. That day the rest of our gear was palletized to be shipped into zone to us after the initial clear. I can't remember at this point what happened, but the mission didn't go off. I remember some bus trouble and ultimately, we ended up back in a GP tent waiting an extra day. That night was miserable for me because it was cold and all I had with me to stay warm was the tarp poncho. I used it to cover up with throughout the night and I woke up gasping for air and covered in condensation. The poncho being airtight had built up condensation where I was breathing under it all night and steadily dripped back on me as I slept. When I awoke, I was freezing cold and had damp clothes. I didn't get back to sleep for the next three days.

It was the 13th of February at about 0130 when we made our way from the staging area to the LZ on Leatherneck to execute our mission. It took several minutes to load all the sticks onto the birds. Then the birds had to conduct their final flight checks, which consisted of lifting off the ground about 20 feet and then hovering, then sitting back down on the pad. It seemed like we did this many times, which sucked. We went up, we sat down. We went up and turned left, we sat down, and so on and so on. I suppose with all the anticipation it made it seem like forever, but that's not it; every man loaded the bird with his pack on his back.

With the average pack weighing about 100 to 120 pounds even sitting, your shoulders begin to get sore quickly. Several Marines also had additional gear such as shoulder-fired rockets,

LIONS OF MARJAH

Claymore mines and anti-personnel obstacle breaching systems (APOBS). An APOBS is a two-pack system each weighing over 50 pounds, used to clear a safe lane of travel for ground elements. This two-pack system fires a small rocket attached to a line charge with 108 fragmentation grenades in it. This will clear a 45-meter by one-meter path.

Finally, after what had seemed like forever, we lifted off the pad and flew into the night. My bird included the Fire Support Team (FST), some explosive ordnance disposal (EOD) attachments and my platoon sergeant, Staff Sergeant Wright. Wright would be the first off and then me. Being the first off the bird meant Wright and I loaded last, putting us right on the door. We were in Army Chinooks CH-47 style. These birds have ramp doors out the back that lift and lower. The bitch of it is that when the ramp is lowered all the way you still have about 24 inches from the ramp to the ground. This is something that you may not be thinking about when you are in a hurry trying to disembark the aircraft.

Ever since the operation order was given all I could think about was getting my guys off the bird quickly and moving to building ALPHA to establish our foothold. Once there I would be able to regroup and breathe a bit. From the entire flight through the brisk night air it was all I could think about. Get them off the bird and to the foothold, off the bird and to the foothold, get to the foothold. As the flight continued longer and longer the lights from Camp Leatherneck faded and the ground went black. I could feel my heartrate start to increase dramatically as the anticipation was rising. This would be the culminating event of my life to this point and possibly ever. Even through all the anticipation and the nerves I was able to calm myself down a little by just looking at the landscape below. It was beautiful; it could almost, at that very point in time, pass for a nice place to visit. Because I was by the door, I could see everything. I remember at one point looking out to where the earth met the sky and distinctly noticing that I could see thousands more stars than ever before. For some reason this brought me a sense of peace. Just at that moment the crew chief signaled that we were two minutes out. "Game Time." I shifted to the edge of my seat and prepared to disembark the chopper.

As the chopper descended toward the earth, I felt my heartrate skyrocket. I flipped down my PVS 14s (night vision device) and stood up behind SSgt. Wright. As the bird put down, there seemed to be an excessive amount of debris in the air. Everything slowed way down for me which seemed odd. This is the altered speed of the mind which is common and is called tachypsychia. For someone affected by tachypsychia, time perceived by the individual either lengthens, making time seem like slow motion, or the opposite, it speeds up, making objects contrast and pass like a speeding blur. For me everything felt like slow motion for the first few minutes of the drop. As soon as the bird touched down, Wright was stepping off the ramp, with me right on his ass. Then the shit hit the fan. I ran right into the back of him. I remember thinking, *What the fuck is he still doing in front of me, he was supposed to buttonhook out and start the perimeter?* We had practiced it about 1000 times in the last few days. That's when I realized that the excessive debris in the air was in fact water and the LZ I just stepped off the bird onto was a flooded poppy field. I landed on top of SSgt. Wright and the rest of the stick on top of us both. The Taliban had flooded the fields expecting our arrival, presumably.

Picture 48 Marines all piled up in a muddy damn mess that's only about 15 meters by 15 meters. Misery started to set in. Welcome to the suck, as they say. Not only was this a flooded poppy field but it was literally swallowing my Marines. Before I knew it, I was about knee-deep trying to trudge out of this mess, all the while trying to keep my rifle clean enough to fire. Of the almost 50 Marines on my stick, SSgt. Wright, Cpl. Bennett, my point man Wetzel and I were the only ones to make it out of the mud initially and get to dry ground. Dry ground was only about 15 meters in any direction from the center of the mud hole; not your textbook insert. Once on the ground I started to get my bearing back and time began to speed up considerably.

Everything happened so fast, but I remember the bird finally taking off after the last Marine disembarked. As I watched him pull up into the night sky there were tracers from enemy fire coming from the ground to the sky all over. I also saw several IR canisters dropped from an AC-130 gunship in a couple of huge circles illuminating the whole area of operation (AO). This was something that to this point in my career I had not seen before. That same AC-130 would be the bearer of bad news about 20 minutes later.

We were scuffling and slopping in the mud trying to be quiet, when all of a sudden over the radio the AC-130 calls down and says:

"Kilo 2-2 be advised; you have a platoon-sized enemy element closing on your position from the north at 300 yards."

"Kilo 2-2 they have small arms and rockets moving toward you from hay bale to hay bale."

See, normally, this would not have been a huge issue but given the fact that we were stuck in the mud and that the radio was on blast, it presented an issue. My entire squad plus reinforcements heard this transmission. That's when panic set in for many, including the Fire Support team leader. A lieutenant, who was likewise stuck, cried out at the top of his lungs, "We're all going to die!"

This was followed directly by SSgt. Wright telling him, "Shut the fuck up Sir!" followed by a brief slap to the face to sure him up proper.

So, as I'm trying to get my squad to quietly set up a defensive perimeter, I feel a hand on my leg. When I looked down, I realized that it was our air officer. He looked up at me with tears in his eyes and said, "Sgt. Rogers, can you help me? I am stuck."

With a quivering chin and tears in his eyes, I could tell that the fear of God was in this man. After helping the captain to his feet, I continued to set up a hasty perimeter around the LZ. With the aid of Staff Sergeant Wright and Cpl. Bennett, we contained the fear that was even in me the best we could and decided we would call in for air support to mitigate the threat before all hell broke loose. When we called for the air support, we were notified that there was a section of Cobra Gunships on station and they would be pushing to our position. As the attack choppers were

RYAN N. ROGERS

pushing from the battle position (BP: a pre-designated area in the sky for choppers to hold until called in for support), I caught a glint in my NVDs of what looked like a firefly. A firefly is an infrared (IR) strobe that runs on batteries. We were given these fireflies to mark friendly positions during the push. As soon as I saw the strobe it hit me. We had our attached Afghan platoon inserted in a Black Hawk just to the north of my position a few hundred meters. They had no communications with us to this point, but the plan was for them to activate their firefly as soon as they touched down in the LZ and make their way south to my position for link-up. The fear of annihilating a friendly force, my friendly counterparts, damn near paralyzed my body. Just as choppers came into zone to commence their gun run, they were called off. ABORT! Had the choppers gone ahead with the gun run it was sure to be an international incident rooting at my incompetence.

Now, a half hour or so in the LZ, our situation started to improve. We had almost gotten everyone unstuck and started to mine sweep a path to get out of the field. I remember the whole time in the LZ, Lt. Emmanuel was contacting SSgt. Wright asking for a SITREP, wondering where the hell we were and why we hadn't reached the foothold for link-up. I'm not sure on the exact dialog of these transmissions but it was something along the lines of "sorry Sir we are stuck in the fucking mud!" As we began to move out, yet another catastrophe struck. My M249 gunner Vuocolo worked his way out of the mud and up to my position and told me, "Sgt. Rogers, I can't find my backpack. I had it on when he came off the bird, but then I fell back first into the mud and had to take it off to get up as it was weighing me down. Can you help me find it?" Though time was already pressing, I went to the spot where he was stuck previously to help him look for it. After about 10 minutes of wading through the mud with no luck I made the decision that we would have to abandon the pack. That is when he told me that he was carrying two white phosphorous 60 mm mortars and a dual-purpose SMAW rocket in his pack. This was not something I felt comfortable leaving in the field without consulting SSgt. Wright beforehand. Leaving that kind of munitions in the field gives the enemy something to use against us and God forbid we need it at some point and don't have it. At first SSgt. was like *fuck no, go find it*. But as time was crucial already, I made my point to him that it would be safer to go to the foothold and then at first light return with metal detectors to find the pack. SSgt. Wright was still not feeling it, called and covered his bases with LT about it. LT agreed that we should go back at first light and told us to make our way to his position.

Now on the move again, I had LCpl. Wetzel my point man for the squad up front mine sweeping a route to LT's position. Because the intel brief was so adamant about the improvised explosive device (IED) threat, I always wanted to have mine sweepers up front. This in the first few hours became annoying. The metal detectors were picking up metal like they were supposed to, but because there was so much trash in that God-forsaken country, the detector would literally go off everywhere you turned. I was so annoyed that when it came down to crossing some of the footbridges that we had to use, I would just say *fuck the detector* and cross first. Now don't get it twisted, I was freaked out on the first one. I edged up to the crossing and stretched my foot out and tapped the ground, hoping I wouldn't explode. When I didn't, I exhaled and then laughed and then crossed the bridge. Every Marine finds his own way to deal with the stressors of combat; my way was typically humor. After a few hundred meters of sweating bullets we could see the firefly on LT's building and made a beeline for it. We conducted our "far recognition" to ensure it was our friendly forces by IR flash in our NVDs. Once link-up was complete we entered the compound to find 1st and 3rd Squads all accounted for. Not only were they accounted for and already on post, but they were just as dry and clean as the moment they boarded the choppers. As you can imagine, my squad did not have the same look.

First Contact

After meeting up with the lieutenant the sun started to come up. My boys found a freshwater well inside the courtyard, so we began to clean weapons. SSgt. Wright came up and told me I needed to take a team and go link up with our Afghani squad and bring them back to the compound, as they were still a few hundred meters north. Even though I didn't like the thought of leaving the comfort of the foothold I rounded up Cpl. Charette's team and off we went. We only had to move a couple of hundred meters which still put us under the overwatch of our machine gunners so that was nice. Having machine gunners in overwatch always gave me a warm and fuzzy feeling. We made link-up with the Afghani squad and made our way back to friendly lines, leaving out the would-be Cobra gun run when chatting with Wundi. At this point it was near 0800. The sun was up and there was an eerie feeling in the air. Our compound was located on a main road intersection. We called the roads 605 and Elephant (608). Skirting 605 was a canal that was about 10 to 20 feet wide depending on the location and we estimated anywhere from eight to 12 feet deep. Elephant was the main supply route (MSR) into a more built-up portion of northern Marjah that was then called Camp Allen. Later this place would be called Camp Hanson. We were on the north side of 605, meaning we would have to cross the 605 canals. As we looked at the map, we figured we were about three clicks or 3,000 meters from Marine Expeditionary Brigade (MEB) Objective 2. This was the objective that our company and then ultimately my platoon had been tasked with seizing. It was a series of compounds that made up a bazaar (or marketplace) with a significant land bridge en route to Elephant. In the vicinity of the land bridge was a suspected master bomb maker's home. We were tasked with seizing the land bridge and destroying any and all threats in the area; however our first task was to set into our foothold and conduct overwatch for 3rd Platoon as they cleared a small village called Shinnywal.

LIONS OF MARJAH

Shinnywal was a moderate-sized village for the area that had somewhere in the ballpark of 80 compounds. Most compounds were small, all made of mud, and most had a courtyard surrounded by a compound wall. The compound walls are typically six to 12 feet tall and 12 to 36 inches thick. Thirty-six inches of hard, packed and sun-dried walls cannot be penetrated by our traditional small arms weapon systems. This becomes an issue when clearing such a structure, because to soften a building requires rockets or heavy weapons. In addition to the situation already being shitty, most of the villages we came across to include Shinnywal were interconnected. This meant that they had small doors that would lead from one compound to another and then to another. Some had alleys that connected the compounds; others would connect from courtyard to courtyard. When these types of villages are hostile it gave the enemy the ability to maneuver through the whole village without exposing themselves. First Platoon was tasked with the clearing of Shinnywal, to set the conditions for us to move on MEB Objective 2. Our first priority was to overwatch 1st Platoon as they cleared, and to mitigate any enemy reinforcements or threats that may present themselves.

From our foothold building we could overwatch 1st during the clear. As the sun came up and things in the area seemed to settle the clear began. From our overwatch position, we spotted two IEDs on the land bridge on 605 that we would have to use to reinforce 1st Platoon if the situation arose. The lieutenant called me on the radio as I was setting my squad into security in the building adjacent to his and told me he needed my EOD attachments and an APOBS. As I made my way over to his compound, I knew he was going to want us to blow an APOBS shot over the IEDs on the bridge. This would hopefully sympathetically detonate the IEDs and give us an unobstructed, IED-free path across the bridge. Just as I thought, LT gave me the plan and I headed out with a small security team made up of LCpl. Grimes's team and my EOD technicians SSgt. Butterfield and SSgt. Stannard. As the two techs discussed the angle of the shot and whether or not the bridge's structural integrity would withstand the blast, it was noticed that command wire was running from the IEDs back toward us and into a compound just south of ours. LT and some other security Marines moved out to clear it, silently hoping to find a trigger man inside to greet with some 5.56mm NATO ball rounds The security team cleared the building, finding nothing but the command wire running to a D cell battery. Though LT wanted the EOD to level the building the command wouldn't sign off on it, so it was back to the APOBS shot.

Just as we were unpacking the APOBS, shots rang out! It sounded like at least one automatic weapon, maybe two. Immediately I moved my element back to cover and took up a defensive posture on the north wall of my compound. There just happened to be a notch in the corner of the compound on the north wall that would provide a perfect firing platform for one to two shooters. Using a pile of dried-up poppy stems I made my way up to the notch and called up Cpl. Simmering with his M249 light machine gun. As we scanned the fields and tree lines to the north, which was where the fire originated, I caught a glimpse of a man with an AK47-type weapon running north at about 300 meters. Without hesitation I raised my M4 and fired. My first two shots were low, as I observed the impacts kick up dust at the fighter's feet. I was wrong on my range estimation, so I adjusted my shot using my 400-meter reticule in my rifle combat optic (RCO) and fired again. This time I would watch the fighter jolt to the side and fall face first to the ground. As he reached out for his weapon, I hit him again with another series of rounds. Just as I came out of my optic there was a second target that appeared in the vicinity of the first, wielding what appeared to be a Soviet Bloc medium machine gun. I directed Cpl. Simmering with his 249-squad automatic weapon (SAW) to the target and called out a range of 400. Just as directed, Simmering fired a fierce 12- to 15-round burst, eliminating the target. As the enemy fighter fell to his face Simmering looked up at me with a huge shit-eating grin and a CLP mustache and let out a whoop. It's like you could feel the emotion running through his body. I looked back at him cold, tapped his Kevlar and said, "Nice shot, but it's not over. Keep your eyes peeled."

LIONS OF MARJAH

Tracing the tree line to the north of where the two enemy fighters now lay lifeless, I knew they had to be running to somewhere they felt safe. As I searched to the north, the tree line ran right up to a two-story compound with what appeared to be eight individuals standing on the roof. All the individuals were wearing black robes with black turbans, but because they were outside of 500 meters it was hard to tell if they had any weapons. Simultaneously SSgt. Wright who was now with 1st Squad was leading a team to the south of the foothold where shots were also taken from. They would move across an open field of about 100 meters and make entry to clear out the suspected enemy compound. As they moved, the snap of more shots sliced through the air, each time grabbing your undivided attention. I knew that SSgt. Wright and 1st were moving to take down that threat, so I turned my attention back to the eight-man team to the north. Just as I glanced to the north, I heard the distinct sound of a rocket-propelled grenade (RPG). The RPG flew at our compound but missed. Though we were a bit outside the typical range for an RPG, and the fact that the Taliban aren't known as accomplished shots, this rocket was still too close for comfort. I immediately started to gen up (generate) a fire mission to call over to 60s. Sixty-millimeter mortars were rolling attached to us at the time and were co-located with LT in the foothold compound adjacent to mine. I broke out my compass and determined the distance and direction to the target building. It took only a moment and I called my fire mission over to the guns that were at the time being controlled by SSgt. Jeremy Owens. SSgt. Owens was the platoon sergeant for Weapons Platoon; an awesome Marine who is among the best I have served with. The way he treated his Marines with a firm but fair dignity commanded his respect. Just like that day, in that moment, when some Marines started to freeze up, he was cool, calm and collected as he started to take the fire mission into his own hands and delivered rounds on target firing from the hand-held mode.

When I heard the first round leave the tube, I made the mistake of trying to observe the impact through my RCO (rifle combat optic). I knew that I was not supposed to do this, but I did anyway. The reason you don't do this is so that if the round impacts a good distance away from the prescribed area you still see it and can adjust. When the first round impacted, I was in my scope and didn't get a good enough observation on the impact site to make an accurate adjustment. Thus, it took multiple rounds being fired before we got the 60s in the right area, never actually making landfall on the right compound.

As the rounds were being adjusted on target, SSgt. Wright was still leading 1st Squad across an open field to the suspected enemy compound a few hundred meters from the foothold. LT was very precise on what rounds were going where. As I was adjusting fire, I remember SSgt. Wright asked the LT where the mortars were going. He had no clue that we had the group of eight to the north. LT told him that I was adjusting to the north but to be safe he called over the radio multiple times, telling 60s to not fire on the compound with the yellow gate to the west because it was friendlies. After finally getting the enemy to the north suppressed, the decision was made to call in for air support on the compound that 1st Squad was moving on. As the bomber came into zone, LT called and told SSgt. Wright to pull back, that he was in communication with the bird and would be dropping a 500-pounder on the compound. I wasn't even with SSgt. Wright at the time, but I am quite sure the pucker factor went up immensely.

Watching the bomber dropping out of the sky to release his payload was awesome from my vantage point. I watched as he zipped down from the clouds and almost went into a dive. As the jet came level and then banked hard back to the sky, I anxiously anticipated the impact. After a few seconds there was no explosion. Over the radio the pilot and our air officer began to talk. The pilot couldn't confirm his target, so he aborted the drop. Captain Baccus, whose call sign was POSH, requested an immediate re-attack. The pilot confirmed and took a second run at it. Again, the air waved off, and again POSH requested a re-attack. Well, they always say the third time is a charm and it rang true that day. On the third run the ordnance was released and the once enemy-filled compound was reduced to rubble.

LIONS OF MARJAH

Following the air attack the battlefield went quiet for a bit. We call this a lull in the fight. I would conclude many months later that the enemy just didn't understand weapons such as fix wing aircraft (jets), surface-to-surface rockets and long-range weapons. The furthest out they can engage was just over 1500 meters with their machine guns and sniper rifles. We could drop bombs from the air, and fire HIMARS and artillery from distances that exceeded 90 clicks. The HIMARS is a M142 High Mobility Artillery Rocket System. We used HIMARS a few times during the deployment and they were fired from several miles away at Camp Leatherneck.

When there is a lull in the fight we typically use this time to top off our magazines with rounds, clean our weapons and stuff some food in our stomachs. This day, however, there was still much work to be done. We had 1st Squad conduct a Battle Damage Assessment (BDA) of the compound we dropped air on, and LT called me back up to get EOD to finish up planning the APOBS shot. Because it was so cold out and we landed in a flooded LZ I started to have Marines becoming very fatigued. Cpl. Charette and LCpl. Vuocolo became especially fatigued. During the drop they were so stuck in the mud that they both ripped their pants trying to get out. Vuocolo was missing damn near his whole left pants leg from the ankle to this beltline, and Charette was not much better. I was afraid that they were getting too cold and did not want to lose them this early in the push for something stupid like hypothermia. Before I took the EOD techs back out to the bridge, I had the Marines not on overwatch build a fire in one of the rooms and set up a rotation to warm the Marines. It's funny what little things will raise the morale for Marines when they are in a shitty situation.

Taking full advantage of the lull, we went back out to the bridge and started to prep the APOBS shot once again. The feeling of everything being real for the first time was awkward to deal with. I trained my entire life for this moment in the future and now here I was living it. LT made the call to hold off on the shot until the sun started to go down a bit so that we could move under the cover of darkness. However, the APOBS were prepped and ready to go just in case 3rd Platoon had trouble during the last phase of the clearing of Shinnywal. I laid with a security team out on the back side of the canal and watched as the sun faded on day one, awaiting orders to light up the night and remind the enemy that lay in wait that we were still coming.

Just before sunset LT received word from Lt. Franco (3rd Platoon's commander) that Shinnywal was clear and his platoon was commencing set-up of the Company Command Position (CP). This meant that the conditions were set for us to make our movement to the CP for link-up.

Once LT got off the hook with Lt. Franco, he pulled in JT, Hinde, SSgt. Wright and myself.

"Okay boys, we're getting ready to move. We will blow the APOBS shot and then Rogers, your squad will take point and move through the field to the south and link up with 3rd at the CP. Any questions?"

With no questions asked, LT told us to break it down and prep to move.

Because we were only traveling with assault packs there wasn't really anything to pack up. This made the breakdown pretty fast and easy. Once I told the squad to roll it up, the team leaders took control and started to get everyone moving. They broke everything down and prepped the boys to move. Our order of movement (OOM) within the squad was second team, machine guns, first team, mortars, third team.

With everyone ready to move and a small security team providing overwatch, Cpl. Charette's team and I again moved out from the cover of the foothold to escort EOD to the bridge. Once there, we assembled two APOBS almost side by side. Firing both side by side would give us a six- to nine-foot path to cross the bridge free from anything that goes boom. Once the systems were set, I called back to LT for the final go-ahead.

"LT, we are set here."

Instantly he shot back with, "Let it rip, Sgt. Rogers."

With the go-ahead we popped smoke for both systems simultaneously and pushed back across the street to take cover in a small ditch. These things make a hell of a boom and send shrapnel for several meters when they blow. Once you initiate the rocket for the APOBS you have seven seconds before the rocket launches. Then, it's an additional seven seconds from launch until the line charges explode. Therefore, we got back to the ditch as fast as possible. As soon as the rockets took off, I could tell the shots were perfect. The first line landed on the left of the IED and the second a few feet to the right. Just as we planned, the charges exploded simultaneously, sympathetically detonating not only the IED that we could see on the bridge but a second that we did not see. The secondary was buried a few meters away from the primary. This was a pretty routine thing that the Taliban would do when burying IEDs. They will often place an IED in the open to grab your attention, hoping that you don't notice the secondary and tertiary IEDs that they conceal all around it. Many times, this has worked in their favor. For us in that place, on that evening, we made the right decision.

Now that the easy part was done it was time to move. In our intelligence brief from higher before the operation kicked off, we were told of an open field that we would have to cross to move into Shinnywal toward the objective. It was briefed that this open field used to have a ton of activity and act as a market area for the locals. However, in the days leading up to the assault, no activity was picked up off any of the regular local populace and it was feared that the once-marketplace was now being used as a minefield full of IEDs. That open field was what we now had to cross under the cover of darkness to link up with 3rd Platoon and the Company CP.

As I called out to my squad to move out, I thought about the night that we had planned for this crossing back on Camp Dwyer with LT. Just after the intel brief prior to leaving Dwyer, LT had summonsed JT, Hinde and me to his hooch to hash out some final plans. When we arrived at his rack, he and SSgt. Wright were studying the Grid Reference Guide (GRG) map of the insertion point and foothold compounds. A GRG is simply a blown-up satellite image of the ground. It shows decent details of the roads and houses, as well as macro and micro terrain from real-time. Using a GRG map versus a one and 25,000 or one and 50,000 map aids in quick acquisition of an area, as well as providing a more detailed look at what terrain you will actually be operating on. It also will have names to all the roads and numbers to all the houses and compounds. So instead of just calling out a would-be grid location on the map to ID a building, you simply call out the section you are referring to and the building number on the map. Whomever you are talking to looks at their map and will find it immediately. As we gathered around the map, the main topic was how to mitigate the open field between our foothold and Shinnywal. LT said, "Alright gents, we have two COAs (courses of action)."

"COA 1, we take our chances with the IEDs and push through the field with metal detectors up front, marking a path with IR chem lights for the rest of the platoon."

"COA 2, we head south on 605 for almost a click and cross on the south side of Shinnywal, then patrol up the back side to link up with the CP."

"What do you guys want to do?"

For JT and me it was a no-brainer. "We take our chances with the field, Sir. Run the metal detectors up front and use IR chem Lights [glow sticks] to mark the path."

LT looked down at his hands, paused and turned to Hinde and asked, "What do you think, Hinde?"

"Sir, I don't like it. I think we take COA 2 and stay on 605 to the south. I have a bad feeling about crossing the other way."

I could tell Hinde was a bit shaken about crossing using COA 1 but at the same time I didn't like walking down the road for a click knowing that I had a 12-foot canal of rushing water on one side and compounds of unknown nature on the other. After we hashed it out for an hour or so weighing the pros and cons of each course of action, we all came to an agreement that we would cross using COA 1, even though I knew Hinde still wasn't a fan.

As these thoughts instantly ran through my head, I began to see my squad filing out of the foothold and heading in my direction. My point man Wetzel was less than thrilled, to say the least, but he took point and broke out his metal detector. To make him feel a bit better about his situation in life I jumped in the file right on his ass and helped him navigate, dropping IR chem lights along the way. As I looked back it was a snaking line of glowing dots on the ground that only were visible in NVGs.

As we moved through the field there was dead silence. It was so cold that the top layer of sand on the ground had a bit of frozen condensation to it, so the only sounds you could hear were the soft, crunchy footsteps of boots on the deck. About a third of the way through the trek Wetzel stopped abruptly and brought his weapon to his face. He was pointing right in front of him at what appeared to be the silhouette of a man. My heart stopped, and I drew my weapon up as well. You couldn't see shit, there was no ambient light that night, so you couldn't make out figures until you were right on top of them. With my weapon raised I could feel my heart now beating through my chest and pulsing through the carotid arteries in my neck. My eyes pulsated as I decided to use the flashlight on the bottom of my M4 to illuminate the would-be target and take action if needed. As the light came on, Wetzel and I were bearing down on a mud pillar in the middle of nowhere. It must have been a piece to an old building or something. Instantly relieved, we exhaled, laughed a little bit and continued to move. After about 35 minutes and 500 meters, the buildings of Shinnywal started to come into view through the NVGs. The closer we came to the town the better I began to feel. I felt better because I knew we were getting closer to friendly forces and would soon link up and be under their overwatch. Once we closed to within 200 meters, I told Wetzel to halt and halted the platoon behind me. At that point I conducted a near/far recognition with what I believed to be the Company CP. I conducted the near/far recognition and then gave the hand and arm signal to move. As I made my way to the entry point of the Command Position, I saw some friendly faces from 3rd Platoon. At the entry point I turned around, dropped to a knee and started to count my squad into friendly lines. Once all were accounted for, I was led by a buddy of mine from 3rd Platoon, Sgt. Harms, to the area in the courtyard that was designated for my squad to sleep. Once there, I pulled my team leaders in and told them to check the boys well for hypothermia and injury, and then to clean the weapons for a good 30 minutes. As the team leaders got to work on that I got back up with Sgt. Harms and had him show me the ins and outs of the CP; things like where the posts were and entry/ exit points. He also showed me where the radio room was as well as where the rest of my platoon would be sleeping. We smoked a few cigarettes and talked about each other's day one experiences and then called it a night.

When I returned to my squad's berthing area, the boys had just finished cleaning weapons. The team leaders were inspecting them and telling the Marines to get some chow in their stomachs. I sat down by Cpl. Charette and began to clean my M4. We whispered a while about the day and what the future might bring us. After chain-smoking about a half a pack of cigarettes each, Charette drifted off to sleep in mid-sentence. I laughed as I put my weapon back together. As I finished assembling my M4, I got a tap on the shoulder from Cpl. Wilson. He was a friend of mine from the mortar section letting me know that they had to sink the mortar base plates. This meant that they would be firing an illumination mission. They fire two or three rounds in order to sink the base plates into the ground so that the follow-on missions are more accurate. The less the system moves when fired, the more accurate it will be. I told him thanks for the heads-up, and he left. The mortar position was about 15 meters behind my squad's sleeping area. Not giving it another thought, I just finished my chow and laid my head down on my pack. I didn't think to wake all my guys up to tell them because they were getting some much-needed sleep.

Boom... Boom...

Two rounds were in the air and you would have thought that my boys were in the middle of a fight. They all popped up, grabbing their weapons scared shitless. It was then I realized that not telling them about the upcoming fire mission was a dick move and a stupid mistake. They calmed down quickly and were quickly back to sleep. I didn't make that mistake again.

As the night passed on like a blur for me, I continued to chain-smoke Newports and think about what the next day had in store for my boys. I remember praying several times that night, asking God to watch over my guys and whatever His will, let it be done through me, an old prayer I heard a bunch growing up. I watched the stars overhead and blew smoke into the night sky, falling into a "flow state" where I was no longer tired, but instead entirely focused on the task at hand, playing the next day out over and over in my head.

Soon I heard the call for 2nd Platoon squad leaders to come to the CP. As I gathered my things I looked down at my watch and saw that it was already 5 a.m. I hadn't slept the first wink.

Valentine's Day

Walking up to the CP, I was still in a flow state that is hard to describe. I met up with Hinde and JT. I saw SSgt. Wright and the LT standing outside the radio room talking and Joe was having a smoke. It would be daybreak soon and I was assuming we would be moving. As we walked up, I connected eyes with the LT and could feel a FRAGO coming. A FRAGO is a fragmentation order. Unlike the PowerPoint five-paragraph order we received in Dwyer, a FRAGO is an on-the-spot order giving the most basic, almost hip-pocket, intel updates on what is happening and what needs to happen. Basically the five W's: **W**ho, **W**hat, **W**here, **W**hen and **W**hy? This would be the first of many FRAGOs I would receive in the following seven months. A Frag Order makes it easy. You get the commander's intent for your mission and you simply execute. All the essentials are handed to you. If I am told what I am doing, when and where I am doing it, what personnel I am going to have with me and what the purpose for me doing said task or mission is, I'm all set. I may not like it from time to time, but rest assured the task will be accomplished.

Once again, we all five gathered around the map using our faint red-lensed headlamps to illuminate the map. LT pointed out on the map where we were, where 1st Platoon was and where 3rd Platoon would be going. He then tasked us out. He said the order of movement was going to be 3, 2, 1. JT's squad would run point for the platoon. My squad and attachments would follow in trace, and Hinde's squad in the rear. We were to depart friendly lines and patrol east almost a click.

Just over a click to the east was where Lt. Neff and 3rd Platoon were located. They had been dropped just south of there the night prior as I was dumped into a 20-degree flooded field. They had established a foothold that day and would now be a supporting effort (SE), overwatching us on our movement and seizure of MEB (Marine Expeditionary Brigade) Objective 2. Once in IVO (in vicinity of) the area to get a look at the Objective, we would conduct surveillance on the area in an attempt to locate the land bridge and our Objective site. Once the location of the bridge and bomb maker's house was confirmed, we would execute the take-down of the objective. With all key leaders on the same sheet of music we slapped the table on the plan and broke to go inform our squads what would go down. I briefed my squad and then told them to clean weapons one more time and get some chow in their gut. We were expected to have our OBJ seized by the close of business.

As the first rays of sun started to break the horizon of the Afghani desert, we were all set and ready to move. Welcoming the warmth of the sun to warm up the world, you could see your breath and the breaths of everyone else as they exhaled waiting the go-ahead. We were departing lines through the south exit as planned. Because we were second in the order of movement, we didn't get outside friendly lines until the sun was up completely. I remember checking my watch as I stepped out of the door on the south wall of the makeshift CP and noting that it was 20 minutes until 1000.

As we exited the CP, I reminded my Marines to do so very slowly. We would be following LT and 3rd Squad. It was imperative that we get good dispersion from the very beginning as we would be moving exposed to the south. As 3rd opened way up in a staggered column, I led my Marines out of the CP and followed in suit. Straight out of the CP, the formation banged left and started to work east through the open steppe. All I could think about was what we would find at the objective and wondered and/or hoped everyone would remember their assigned tasks during the exploitation phase of the mission. I can only imagine what the Taliban fighters must have been thinking as they watched us pile out of the courtyard and walk into the fight. This morning was much like the new recruiting commercials about running toward the fire.

About 300 yards into the movement, the sound of belt-fed machine guns and RPGs pierced the air. Immediately the sounds of return fire from the awesome and terrifying M240B mixed with the sweet sound of friendly small arms fire and erupted up to the northeast. Following the initial fire, the air was flooded with the sounds of all different weapons systems from all different directions. The intensity level escalated to the max and everyone got a little hitch in their giddy-up. As the anxiousness grew, we were marching straight toward the fire. The key leaders who had radios with them such as SSgt. Wright, all the squad leaders, LT and some of the attachments could hear the chatter from 3rd Platoon who was in contact. Reports of the enemy started to flood both the company and platoon networks. I remember consciously trying to stay calm while continuing the march for 3rd Platoon's location. The way I calmed myself down was to embrace the suck and put a smile on my face. In a situation like this there are a million things going through your head that shouldn't be. There are indeed only a few things that you MUST focus on. First, I had to ensure I took in as much information as possible on the move regarding my terrain, cover, enemy locations, friendly locations, etc. Secondly, I had to be very aware of my surroundings and the signals coming from the front of my own formation. I must first get my squad to the fight for my squad to get in the fight. Knowing that it would only be minutes before we would be able to have eyes on the fight and lend our assistance, I kept calm and signaled for my squad to pick up the pace. We were in a slow jog as we broke northeast to move into some interconnected compounds to link up with 3rd Platoon. It reminded me of the movie "Troy" where Achilles and his men are about to storm the beach. We were lions about to write history on behalf of the greatest republic ever conceived.

Third Platoon was updating us all the way that the enemy was to the south and they were firing mortars, machine guns and rockets. They said the enemy was moving about the area on moped-type vehicles and that they were seemingly accurate with their fires. They also made references to the GRG maps we all were given as to what compounds the enemy was presumed to be firing from. As we closed on the location, thoughts of tactics and the safety of my men raced in my mind. The closer we got to the engagement area, the louder and more intense the gunfight became. I smiled every time I would hear the friendly M240 open up. It has a very distinct sound to it. It's very loud and very fast, sort of cracking the air around you. I smiled partly because I knew that if the 240 was opening up, the enemy was piling up; and partly to calm myself down. Anytime I would find myself overanxious in a situation I would just force a smile and it would ground me. About a hundred yards in front of me now I could see JT and his squad moving into the south entrance of a compound. SSgt. Wright was directing traffic. When I moved up to the compound, the sounds of the gunfire were right on top of us. We had reached the fight. For a few split seconds I remember distinctly noticing how calm all the Marines around me were; not only my squad, but JT's and Hinde's squads as well. It was an amazing thing to experience. Later I would realize that this would not have been possible without the superior leadership and overwhelming calm that both SSgt. Wright and Lieutenant Emmanuel put off. When you see your leadership calm it is calming; when you see your leadership chaotic it can be chaotic. Remember to remain calm.

As I moved up to the compound where JT and SSgt. were, SSgt. Wright directed me to move through JT's squad and take point. I did so quickly with my squad in trace. As I moved through JT's squad to the front, I saw a gap in the wall I was skirting. The gap created an entrance to the courtyard of the compound adjacent to my position. The outer east-facing wall of that courtyard was receiving enemy rounds but was a perfect firing position for my squad if we could get to it. The wall stood about four to five feet tall and was about 30 inches thick. This meant a couple of things to me. First off, my squad would be able to use it for cover while still being able to engage over the top of it. Also, being a thick wall, it would be able to sustain almost any weapons systems that would be thrown at it. Instantly I made the decision to lead the squad up to the wall and start to fight. I echeloned my element by twos and threes up to the wall. I moved up with LCpl. Wetzel initially and realized another great thing about this position. Not only was it 30-plus inches thick of hard, packed mud, it also had a small knee-high wall that ran off it to the east that would be a prime position to fire to the south.

As the whole squad fell in on the wall I looked over and found that I had a "tag-along" with my squad from the media. C.

J. Chivers, a New York Times combat correspondent, was inserted with the company headquarters anticipating the action of day two and ready to capture the day's events both with his handy cam and his pen and paper. I asked him to stay low and out of the way and went about my business.

I moved to an opening in the wall to try to get some observation on the enemy positions. No more did I stick my head out of the opening than I heard *snap-snap-snap* over my head, the sound that incoming rounds from a long rifle make when they are above you which sound just like a small firecracker. It's a very quick, distinct snap, like one of the small white firecrackers you get from the fair as a kid; the type that comes in a small bag or box that are white and have a small string on top. I used to throw them at my buddies' feet on the ground or any hard surface and they'd snap. Hearing the snap in gunfight is just as relieving as it is unnerving. It's an awesome yet horrifying feeling; like "holy shit that's fucking close!" For some, their heart will jump into their throat or miss beats altogether. For others it just pisses us off. Then a relieving calm comes about you because if you hear the snap you know you didn't get hit! I didn't get this feeling all the time. It would usually happen when either I hadn't taken contact in several days or when the fighting was so intense that I started to lose faith or hope of making it out of the fight. In the first days of the invasion of Marjah, it happened a lot.

As the fight pressed on, my SA (Situational Awareness) of the enemy fighters and their positions got better. I was able to get eyes on where the enemy was and where his reinforcements were coming from. From my position all Taliban positions were to the south and southeast. They were at ranges from 450 meters all the way out past a grand. Being that they were to the south primarily I opted to push a team of Marines including Cpl. Jesse Bennett and LCpl. Travis Vuocolo out to the small east and west running wall. They were able to get into a modified prone position utilizing the small wall for cover and begin engaging the Taliban fighters. This day of fighting quickly became aggravating because at the distances we were at, it was sometimes difficult to tell who had weapons and who didn't. The Taliban started to move about the battlefield wielding no weapons and per our rules of engagement we were not be able to fire some of the time. As they would move, we would be fighting with a group of enemy fighters in one compound or another. We would try to have Marines maintain eyes on the individuals moving about but it became quite a task. A few hours into the fight that morning I noticed that the enemy was sending what appeared to be reinforcements through a small irrigation canal to the south about 700 meters from my position. This is a pretty good piece for the average marksman, especially at moving targets. I had my squad as well as the squad of Afghan Army counterparts that were attached to me before the pushback on Camp Dwyer. One of the Afghan soldiers carried an old M240G. His name I could not pronounce but he went by Sadiqu. He was by far the most motivated fighter amongst the ANA that were attached to my squad, and with the M240G I learned that day he was a beast. Upon seeing the squad-sized enemy element of Taliban fighters in the canal to the south I called Sadiqu up to my position, which was a break in the east-facing wall. I was a bit exposed where I was and to not put him into any more danger than necessary Sadiqu was instructed to get into the prone position. Once in the prone, Sadiqu looked up to me as if to ask what I wanted him to do.

"Sadiqu, right over there, Taliban you see?" I asked Sadiqu using my hands and arms. I felt like I was back at home playing charades with my brothers again. Sadiqu got the point and searched the area to the south. When he looked back at me, I could tell he was clueless. He shook his head and said "No Talib."

"Yes Sadiqu!" I got down into the prone position beside him and grabbed his Kevlar helmet. With a bit of a jerk I did my best to aim his eyes directly to where the fighters were exiting the canal. Suddenly the soldier postured up tensely and I knew he could see the target, kind of the same way a dog will perk up when a cat runs through the yard. It was as though I could feel the excitement run through his eyes into his brain and then to the rest of his body. His body was firing all the signals that one's body fires off when about to engage. I popped to a knee immediately. I am still not sure what he said but he looked up at me and spoke. It was something to the effect of "yes I see them now," only it was in Pashtunwali, which was the dialect of Arabic the soldiers there spoke.

"Shoot?" he asked after.

"Yes shoot, shoot now, Sadiqu!"

Instead of the Afghan soldier dropping back down into the prone where the weapon is the easiest to control and in turn most accurate, he popped to a knee and manned the weapon up to his right shoulder. The soldier then took a few strides to the small wall that Vuocolo and Bennett were on and remained in the kneeling position. I didn't even have time to shout an ADDRAC before he ripped out the first of about six or eight medium-sized bursts with the machine gun, one after another.

I couldn't be sure of how many fighters Sadiqu personally killed with the six or eight bursts he fired; however, all of them went down and none of them got up. There were several other Marines, Corpsman and ANA on the field that could have contributed to the elimination of the enemy in that ditch, but I am quite certain that most of them were due to the man we called Sadiqu.

Unfortunately, as the day pressed on, the enemy began to learn our ROEs. They started laying their weapons down in the house they were shooting from and then moved on motorbike to a new house with no weapon present. So, while moving, we can't engage unless we are 100 percent sure it's a combatant, which at range is hard to do. They would get to the new platform, be it a building or alleyway, and then we would begin to receive rounds from that direction. Chaos was in full swing and we were faring well. As the enemy reinforced, they began to flank us to the east quietly. With Marines exposed to the east, the enemy opened up once more, this time from the east. Rounds were snapping by our heads in every direction as I yelled for the Marines to peel out from the end and get back behind the wall. As Vuocolo got up with his ripped frog pants and ran toward me, the enemy was all over us. The other two teams really laid down some suppression now from the wall to match the Taliban's fire rate. With the whole peel taking only seconds all teams were now safe and suppressing the enemy. Cpl. Bennett called out that they had a sniper firing, and that he was getting closer and closer. As my squad fought the enemy squad, the fight raged. Snaps and ricochet zips filled the air, mixed with the already blown-out ears and the high-pitch tinnitus that comes with it. I was on the right side of the opening in the wall when I called for LCpl. Grimes to come forward with his M203 grenade launcher. I wanted him to mark the building that we were receiving sniper fire from. He loaded a green ground-marker 40mm into the tube and took aim. I needed this marker in order to get a proper and accurate shot from a vector dagger laser pointer. That was the system required to mark a building that we wanted to send indirect fires to hit. Just as the smoke began to billow, the sniper and his posse opened up once more, peppering the side of our wall and gaining our full attention once more. With the smoke on the deck and bullets flying, I ran back about 45 meters to the opposite wall to get the Fire Support team leader to shoot the vector dagger shot. I showed him my smoke and hauled ass back to my wall.

Once the vector dagger shot was made the coordinates were submitted to higher headquarters for them to generate a fire mission on that spot, in case we needed to reduce the building in the future. Back with my squad the fight continued. I was going up and down the line yelling out "only shoot what you can hit." As bullets were whizzing by left and right the call went up. "Corpsman Up!"

I never wanted to hear those two words in my life outside of training. As Doc Fowler rushed over to the downed man, I was right behind him crossing the gap in the wall to reach him as bullets rained in on us. The wounded man was LCpl. Travis Ford Vuocolo. He had been shot through the left shoulder. Doc instantly started to treat the wound and wrap V's arm up, and I began to get his medical tag information in order to call him in a casualty evacuation report. I wanted to get him out of there as fast as possible, knowing that it may be later than sooner. As I was collecting data, LCpl. Mackiewicz, in a fit of rage while screaming you "mother fuckers," emptied what seemed like half of a magazine or so over the wall at the enemy. He blew off his steam and regained his composure.

I called over to LT and SSgt. Wright letting them know I had a man hit and that I wanted to level the fucking building he got hit from. With the vector dagger shot already made, requests went up. Eventually after several more minutes of banging it out with the Taliban, two "sonic booms" erupted in tight succession, and then two explosions in the same succession. It was the single most violent and impressive display of firepower I had ever called for or witnessed. It leveled the building. But it leveled the wrong building. It leveled a building 300 meters to the north of the building I took sniper fire from and the building that I had Grimes mark with his smoke. I am not sure where the break in communication was or how the wrong compound got called in, but something went terribly wrong. When the rockets impacted, the entire battle space went silent. They again couldn't understand long-range weapons like this. After a breath or two of silence, the horrid sound of women and children making gut-wrenching screams penetrated the air. As they poured out of the rubble, some still on fire, I watched through my RCO, some with legs, some not; some with arms, some not. I couldn't tell how many there were but knew it was bad.

Instantly there was a mass casualty mission generated and sent to higher for support, and the CO ordered another squad to go assist on the ground in any way necessary for the evacuation. As the squad stared across the open steppe, the enemy again opened. The Marine squad made contact at the rocket site and needed a bird down fast. With the mission already moving up the ladder it wasn't long before air was on station and descended toward the earth with their escort birds banking 90 degrees sideways and laying in some 50-caliber love to the fight below. The evacuation bird moved in for a landing to get the local women and kids off the field and to higher help when a Taliban fighter launched an RPG from underneath it. I can remember thinking we were going to be in another "Black Hawk Down" situation when by the grace of God and amazing pilot skills, the bird got away from what looked to be a sure hit. With the near-miss logged into the books, the hopes of landing and getting these people out of there fast enough was fading by the second. A total of seven women and five small children were killed as results of their injuries from the rocket attack.

It was a blow to both the local populace and to the Marines on the field. Nobody wants to kill women and kids, and nobody wants to make more enemies out of our mistakes. However, to believe we can have a gentleman's war and only the soldiers die and no civilian casualties occur is to believe in fairytales. At that time in my life, I was not shaken by this moment. It would have a much different effect on me later.

The rockets silenced the battlefield and gave us some time to recollect what had taken place. We used the lulls to communicate and reload our weapons systems and carry out the casualty evacuations of the dead and wounded.

Shortly after I radioed V's CASEVAC into SSgt. Wright, he began to make his way to me. For a platoon sergeant in combat, that is their wheelhouse all the way: call in air support and fire support, and 2Bravo was second to none. He was so good it even rubbed off on the guys. When he came into view, he was smoking a Marlboro Red and carrying his write-in-the-rain notebook ready to record some data for the bird, no doubt. He started to move through and check on the boys and I then came to V and started asking him some routine questions. He informed me that when I called in V's CASEVAC I had labeled the wound as urgent surgical. This moves him to top priority to be scooped up. It was not urgent surgical, and I was corrected. This was a mistake that could really cause someone with a graver injury to be picked up later than necessary, resulting possibly in death. At the time I just wanted my guys to get care immediately.

The Black Hawk from "Dustoff" came into zone and was communicating with 2B when I launched a yellow smoke onto the field in the area designated clear for them to land. The pilot confirmed the smoke to 2B and descended rapidly to the earth, placing the smoke canister promptly between his skids, swirling the smoke into the blades as the crew chief jumped down and opened his arms telling us it's good to come on. Just before he took Vuocolo from me like a hand-off, V looked at me in the eyes and said, "I don't wanna get on the chopper!" He'd just seen how close they were to being blown out of the sky and didn't want to risk it. I tapped him on the shoulder and said, "You're getting on that fucking bird, let's go." He jumped up on the bird with his butt and scooched over and inside. As quickly as they had come down to the earth, they were back up and off once more. I felt great that V was on the bird but had my guys dividing up his ammo for the fight to come. We kept his weapon as well, an M249 Squad automatic weapon. It was one of the three most vital weapons to my squad. It had to be retained and reissued out.

As Valentine's Day started to move to night, I had never welcomed the darkness so much. I needed a mental reprieve that could only come by way of relaxation and sleep, both of which I hadn't gotten any of to this point. We would be getting orders shortly to hardpoint a specific area but were to remain at the wall until then. Everyone was completely smoked as day two closed to the darkness.

- With war there will always be collateral damage, the grunt doesn't welcome this, but he understands it. At least he understands it as it pertains to his current situation. The situation of life and death with incomplete intelligence. Him or Me.

The Big One

As the company consolidated on night two, the COC (Company Operations Center) would remain in the original building from the night prior and the individual platoons would now be setting up their own battle positions or BPs. I had to give up one of my Marines to the company for the first sergeant's quartering party. This was a routine thing that everyone had to participate in, and I would have my boys back with me the following day or so. I chose Minime and Simmering. They left with radio batteries and other odds and ends, and the remainder of my squad and attachments were spread out in a defensive posture, posted up awaiting word from the top. After a short period of time the key leaders were called up to LT's position to discuss options. When I arrived at the CP, I was greeted with a fresh American Newport cigarette from Herby. He was a key leader as well as a machine gun squad leader. The LT commenced and after action of the day's events, gave each person a chance to speak out on anything they might want to bring up. He was truly an amazing leader. Hinde brought up that he had seen some large OE-style antennas coming out of some hardened-looking structures up by what appeared to be the land bridge and bazaar that was referenced in the operation order. This became the primary concern of the conversation and Hinde had already posted men on watch, to report back with any movement. With the primary objective tentatively identified, the plans were simple. We were to take up position under the cover of darkness close to the objective. My squad was tasked out with moving to, clearing and securing a building that was less than 300 meters from our current position and less than 300 meters from the OBJ site as well.

After the table was slapped on the plan, I was sick to my stomach. To this day I'm not sure why, maybe it was nerves, maybe it was the thought of facing my squad knowing that I was just as scared (if not more scared) than they were, and talking to them about what was to come next. I couldn't seem to get Vuocolo out of my head either, or his father. It was almost 45 days to the day when I shook this man's hand and he placed his son's life in my hands, and now he had a hole in his arm and was removed from my control. One thing I took solace in was the last thing V's father told him was to "kill em good;" well, he did exactly that. He got the hole in his arm patched up and then I told him to post back up. Without hesitation this man became a lion once more and threw that saw up on the wall and laid down some hate and discontent. I told him to make them pay for that hole in his arm and he did just that.

Once I was back to my position, I called up my team leaders and briefed them on the plan. I told Bennett he would be taking point and showed him the compound I wanted to take. We would be moving out in 30 miles and the team leaders went to brief their men. Whenever I was speaking to my Marines, I never showed fear. There were many times I was probably more afraid than they were, but I tried to maintain a level head. Sometimes I could compose myself and sometimes I couldn't. Being that it was day three coming we were running low on food. The order stated that we were to have the OBJ in 24 hours and the ground line of communication (GLOC), which is our ground supply routes, should be open already, and they weren't. With the food supply running low I briefed the team leaders to eat only what was necessary for energy. I had been rationing my grub from the onset; not because I'm some sort of saint, but because I literally couldn't eat. I couldn't eat or sleep to this point in the push. The little food I did force down made me nauseous. I gave out three main meals to the boys who were out and told them they could eat after we secured the foothold.

After checks were good and everyone was ready, we began to echelon out of the current compound en route to the new foothold and potential BP. As we approached the compound everything was quiet and dark. Through the NVDs as we approached, I could see off in the distance the land bridge and the hardened structure Hinde had referenced with the antennas. I could only imagine that we would be in a gunfight in this very spot soon. The first team entered the courtyard, followed by me and then Team 2 and 3 who were combined at this point due to the loss of V, and Minime and Simmering with the quartering party. Following them was the ANA-attached squad led by Wundi Guall and then the machine gunners. The courtyard was large and rectangle-shaped, with multiple outhouses for animals and what seemed to be storage buildings. The people here also live with their families for much longer than Americans do, and they have many more children, it seems. There may be 20 some people living in one compound. It's disheartening to see how some people live.

Inside the courtyard wall is where you find the living huts and animal quarters. In this courtyard, there was a large circular walled-in, corral-type area with what I can only describe as a mini "circus tent"-like tarp, held to a single, tall pole in the middle. It was also secured to the corral walls, offering a shitty situation to clear out but an awesome shield from the elements once you owned it. The clear, though nerve-racking, went smooth, silent and without a hitch. Once secure, I communicated with the other squads and LT, letting them know that the conditions were set for them to move.

After the consolidation was complete, all of second platoon and the attached elements were massed and setting the plan for one last push to secure the MEB OBJ 2. All the key leaders were consolidated in one of the living quarters discussing the events of the following day. The platoon's small unit leaders set up radio and post watch rotations and bedded the Marines down. Being that the compound was hardened and rectangular made it easy to defend. At this meeting it was mentioned that many of the Marines were low on both food and water. This was relayed to the company command and they advised all Marines to conserve water. This meant no more shaving until further notice. Nobody was comfortable using even the iodine tablets to purify the wadi water, as we all witnessed the locals both bathing and shitting in it. No shaving was a small win, and sometimes it takes just enough small wins to get a unit through hell. They also advised us that the following day the trucks should be opening the GLOC and our food would be here. Another small win.

As LT assessed the situation we again took to the map with our red headlamps. We were looking at two large, hardened machine gun bunkers, both mutually supporting one another with a space between them of about 50-100 meters. They backed up against the bazaar and one could only guess they would have fun little treats buried all around it, as we were given intel in our first brief that this was a master bomb maker's home. The idea was to fix and flank using an action right movement. My squad was tasked with being the support by fire element. We were to fix the enemy on ourselves and lay hell into them, while the other two squads assaulted up and then made an action right sweeping through the OBJ. The bazaar stretched both east and west running past the bunkers, so it would be a long sweep and clear. I would have one squad of machine guns attached to me as well as my ANA who were equipped with both machine guns and RPGs. We didn't know it that night but the next morning we would be in one of the hardest fights of our lives.

All of us took a second to gather our thoughts and work out how we wanted to task out our own individual elements the next day. Everyone probably has their own style or way of building a mission order, but for me it always seemed terrifying. My platoon sergeant would always say that about me, "Dude, you're one of the best I have seen once you're in the shit, but you're a coward when it comes to the planning phase." I used to take that personally and get offended when he would say it; now I look at it as a compliment. I am not a fan of planning an attack or a mission where my friends and Marines may die. It scares me. When I'm in the action phase there is no choice in the matter, it's just time to go to work, earn that check. With the plan in my head I called my team leaders up and briefed them. I explained how we would be a base of fire and I showed them a small, waist-high wall about 200 to 250 meters from the bunkers to the direct front. This is where we would fight as the other squads advanced. Getting there should be relatively easy so long as we don't wake up to a gunfight, I told them. I also tasked the machine guns to do whatever they needed to do to best support my mission. They ended up planning to set the two guns up close to the flanks on each side of the base so that they would have intersecting fields of fire and would mutually support one another. This is where they can cover each other's flanks and even fire on one another if a position is overrun. That's a hell of a thing to have to teach a 22- to 25-year-old man, to have to be able to think about and execute in a split second when lives are on the line. What decisions do normal 22-year-old people have to make? I wondered that a lot while in Marjah. I could see some hesitation in the boys' eyes when I briefed them on the plan, but they all nutted up slapped the table and left to clean weapons and get some sleep.

At this point I was so exhausted that I had no choice but to sleep, as badly as I didn't want to. After my radio watch hour expired, I walked the post line one more time and checked on my squad. Once satisfied that all my guys and gear were good, I headed for the corral. The wind had picked up when the sun fell, and the desert got frigid cold. Everyone had wind-burnt faces and chapped lips. I remember looking up at the stars before climbing into the corral and praying a prayer for the first of many times. I prayed that when my time came, whether that was today or tomorrow, that it will be fast and that I won't suffer. I prayed for something like a round to the head or a fast IED death. Not because I am a coward but because I didn't want there to be time for my guys to hesitate, or for them to see me suffer or something of the sort. I ended the prayer as I always did with "let your will be done through me" and I climbed into the animal corral and closed the tarp door behind me. I was freezing cold, wearing wet clothes from sweating all day, and had no sleeping bag or warming layers. "Pack light, freeze at night," as the saying goes. Luckily as I made my way through the bedded-down Marines I found Herby snuggled tight in his black bag. He unzipped and sat up like something out of a scary movie with a big shit-eating grin on his face, knowing that he told me to pack a bag in my kit and knowing that I didn't listen to him. We bullshitted for a few minutes and burned a couple of Newports before both climbing in that same black bag and trying to get a few hours of sleep, the first I had logged in since we woke up the day of the push. It's odd to me how the flow state can get you through some incredible experiences; through the pain of continuing, through the emotional journey of the unknown, and through the motions of your training that matter the most.

In the morning we woke just before sunrise. Under the cover of darkness the Marines of Kilo Company and 2nd Platoon were preparing their weapons for a fight and trying to scrounge the last of any chow they had left. With a three-day beard on all faces we awaited the company commander at our position. He was to be here when the sun came up and it was going to be weird to have my entire unshaven squad be under observation, even if it was at the command's order. When the command showed up, they too had unshaven faces and the first sergeant made a few jokes, ultimately ending with an uplifting talk to inspire the boys, even if it wasn't apparent. Regardless, we all were set to go when the first gunshots broke the morning silence. This came to be normal in the days and months ahead. When the gunfire breaks out things seem to slow down a bit for me. I have a bit of auditory exclusion, which means I hear only what is necessary. I experienced this as a child when I would pitch for my ball team. Everything would slow down and I would only hear the catcher; then as the pitch was delivered, everything silent and everything slow, as soon as the ball hit the glove the world became alive again for me to react to. It was a lot like that for me in a gunfight as well.

With the silence now broken and hate in the air, I communicated with my squad that we needed to hit them hard and soften them, so we could advance to the waist-high wall where we planned to fight. I don't know how many machine guns were shooting at us from the two bunkers, but it seemed like four or more. Each bunker had six catholes cut into them for firing platforms, then they had concrete T-wall barriers for the roofs. They were impressive; way more conventional than any of the houses that were in the area. As we tried to gain fire superiority, I remember thinking, "This is crazy, machine gun bunkers!" Never in my wildest dreams did I think I would be in this type of fight. I was almost grateful that I hadn't missed it, as up until that point we were perfect minus V's through and through. It was everything I wanted.

Snap! Snap! Snap! Back to reality. We had rounds coming in close and we needed to press harder. My squad was on the north courtyard wall now firing into the bunker and the catholes, and the battlespace was erupting all around us as we weren't the only ones engaged. The other platoons were likewise in gunfights as well as our attached snipers. After a short period of time we weren't getting anywhere, so I took the LAW shoulder-fired rocket off Cpl. Charette's back and secured my back-blast area, ensuring I wasn't about to rock someone standing behind me when I fired. I fired the rocket thinking it was going to be a showstopper. The rocket hit directly where it was intended and exploded, to the sight of a huge cloud of dust and sand, and a massive boom. The enemy machine guns answered right back at us, as if to say, "Fuck you, that was weak." Matt was not thrilled about carrying the rocket and not firing it, but time was pressing.

When this happened, we had skids on station circling above. It was a Cobra: a Cobra section of gunships that were more than ready to get called into the fight. They are equipped with some amazing firepower: Hellfire rockets and a heads-up display for the pilot that allows him to engage anything he is looking at with a 30-caliber GAL, which is a six-barrel machine gun that can chew through just about anything, dumping a few thousand rounds almost instantly. As Pistol 46 (the Cobra pilot's call sign) descended on the battle space he was coming from the south and was nose-toward my position. This is the first time I was paralyzed in combat. I literally couldn't move as the GAL opened on the enemy bunker. I didn't realize that bird was pointed at us and the gun at the enemy; I thought we were going to be killed by our own support. Not to mention the terrifying sound of that gun.

As I ran back to the north wall, I remember the choppers being directly above and the brass falling into the courtyard we were in. It reminded me of the movie "Black Hawk Down," when the mini-birds come in for support and rain hot brass down on the army units. When I realized he was chewing the enemy up we made our move for the waist-high wall. I motioned to the team leaders and squad that we were going to be moving, and to pick up the rate of fire. When I say that I motioned, I cannot help but to explain what I mean. I mean the communication that a well-trained, tight-knit squad has is implicit. Meaning looks, whistles and hand and arm gestures can just about handle the job with little to no verbal communication between either party. This comes only after months and months of training together, eating, sleeping and warring together. As I exited the courtyard running north to the new position, I remember running straight for the wall and seeing someone's boots come into view beside me. It was the ANA commander who was rushing to the wall beside me and he had been shot in the face and knocked off his feet. It was like something out of a movie. I remember the shock of it as it happened and was over quickly. I saw too many new amazingly shocking things in such a short period of time that the "give a fuck" got broken.

Once we reached the wall, we started to lay down heavy volumes of fire to keep the enemy fixed. Conditions were now set for JT and Hinde to execute the action right. LT would be moving with them in the assault. With the squad being fought by the team leaders I pulled a few Marines from Charette's team to aid in getting the commander picked up and off the battlefield. Surely it would only take a minute as he was hit in the face. Wetzel and Charette made their way to help the downed commander, as they witnessed him get up and run back to the cover from whence we came.

Matt was amazing when it came to the radios, as he had gone to school for it before we deployed. He learned the ins and outs of being JTAC-certified and it really paid off. SSgt. Wright was able to roll the frequency on the encrypted comms and communicate with the birds to get a CASEVAC in. This is in his job description, but it's an ever-evolving process that most grunts are not familiar enough with that early in their career and to be proficient at it under fire.

Doc Fowler was with Matt's team and in my mind, kept that man alive to see another day. He cared for the commander like he was one of his own squad members and got him on the bird alive. My hat was tipped to my men in that moment. One first deployment corpsman and one second deployment corporal team leader, one 19 and one 21, under fire in the pits of Marjah, had enough training and poise to maneuver under fire and keep the presence of mind and clarity of thought to not only save a life but also coordinate with the birds and complete the evacuation. It's amazing to call them my Marines. Regardless of age, they managed just fine and executed the CASEVAC with our platoon sergeant. The commander was shot in the face just below his cheek bone, and the round exited his head back by his ear. He was hit by a 7.62 mm round fired from a Soviet bloc medium machine gun, firing presumably from the catholes in the bunkers. We would learn later that the commander was back on the battlefield leading his men in just a couple of weeks.

With Doc and Charette back with the squad, we fought on. With 2nd Platoon now being directly supported by what felt like every asset in Afghanistan, we had several people helping us from the air and ground. One of the linguist Marines who spoke the language was monitoring unencrypted nets to see if he could catch any enemy chatter. They were known to utilize handheld radios for communication on the battlefield as well as Nokia cell phones. He intercepted a transmission during the fight that was something to the tune of "hit them with the big one." The information was immediately disseminated across the battlefield and the anxiety grew. Everyone was on the lookout for the big one.

I am not sure exactly how this next part really went down, but this is how I remember it...

As the entire platoon and company were bringing American resolve to the fighters of Marjah and really laying into the machine gun bunkers, a lone mule came running full speed ahead like someone had slapped his ass and said, "Get the Americans!" On this mule's back was some sort of contraption covered in a tarp or blanket. Whatever was under the tarp was about three-foot-high off the mule's back and wider than the mule itself. It was some crazy shit leaning into two machine gun bunkers knowing that there were enemies in there trying to kill you. Next thing you know someone yelled "IT'S THE BIG ONE!" The entire platoon reinforced, all at once turning their fires to the "big one." With multiple machine guns and several small arms bearing down and unloading into the mule, he was not much of a match, but I will say with the amount of firepower he was hit with, he would be in consideration for one of the toughest mules in the world. I felt bad for the animal in hindsight as the contraption on his back was nothing more than a large load of dried-up poppy stems.

Once he was down and the threat of the Big One blowing us all to hell was gone we continued to hit the bunkers. The assault element was now in the first stages of their action right and we were about to close fires on the bunker. It was mentioned later that the snipers had a super advantageous position during the clear phase and were picking fighters off as they began to abandon the bunkers. As LT and the assault element continued the clear, I was to set security and act as a reactionary force for support. I rolled my boys up into a defensive perimeter and we held. All in all, a successful morning thus far. Most of the fighters were killed, but a few remained to act as a cleanup crew. They seemed to be using these white vans as their medical vehicles.

After sitting and getting bored, listening to the radio became a pastime. I liked to listen to the company nets to listen for the voices of my friends and in general for all-around updates. I still had a pair of Marines with the company first sergeant for the quartering party and now was as good a time as any. To this point in time I hadn't taken off my boots yet and could feel my feet becoming raw. I was always a stickler about my guys taking care of their feet and here I was neglecting mine. I decided I would go to the center of the courtyard and take my boots and socks off for some much-needed sun. As I walked out of the makeshift radio room, I threw my plate carrier on and grabbed my Kevlar. Staff sergeant was on the hook with LT when I walked out. I was just in the process of removing my boot bands when I heard Grimes yell at someone to stop and he raised his weapon. He was posted up in the northeast corner of the courtyard on some dried-up stacks of poppy stems from the last opium harvest. I grabbed my M4 and bolted to his position. Right behind myself was Wundi. I told Wundi to talk to the approaching man and stop him or we were going to fire. The approaching man didn't have a weapon on him but was clearly inebriated from something. He was completely out of his mind coming right at us on foot, smiling. When Wundi ordered him to stop, they exchanged words and Wundi looked at me and said, "He not right," pointing to his head. Then I told Wundi that he had to stop, or we had to stop him. I called back to staff sergeant to get a confirmation to shoot this guy if needed and he said we could not shoot. When he said this, I looked at Wundi and said, "It's your fucking country dude, handle this." Wundi pulled up his M16 and fired at the man's feet. The man laughed and flipped us off, turned and began to walk toward the bazaar. Wundi looked at me, laughed and said, "See, he craaaazzzy!" again pointing at his head. We instantly called down to JT and Hinde to inform them of what he looked like and that he was coming, just to be on the safe side. I had a bad feeling about the entire deal, and I knew I should have just shot and killed him. He walked and all I could think about was that he may be trying to hurt my buddies. With the trucks in Lima Company being met with just as much resistance as we were, they were again unable to open the GLOC and we were now out of food, almost completely, and our water was critically low. I had at least two Marines that were ill in my squad and another, LCpl. Mickiewicz, was crossing a wall during the fight the day prior and had injured his shin. It was nothing too bad, so he didn't make much of a gripe about it. He too was seemingly ill, though. We decided they must have contracted dysentery from the dirty canal water and overall "shitty conditions." The elements alone were enough to drive all your will out and then you had to fight all day long. My plans of airing out my feet changed to a fast on and off sock change. I was greeted with bloody socks and raw feet begging for sunlight, but they weren't as bad as they were after the 22-mile trek back at home. We rode the day out holding up post on what was now deemed the Alamo. The team leaders generated a post roster for fire watch and radio watch, and the remainder of the Marines began hardening the position with the sandbags we all packed in under our chest plates in case we needed to stay here another night. Meanwhile, inside the CP, staff sergeant was generating an emergency resupply drop of water and food for not only us but the entire company. The plan was that they would come in under the cover of darkness at around 0230 and drop an Air Force pallet with 10,000 bottles of water and a pallet of MREs as well. Being that it was still daylight at this point, it was a lifetime away.

The assault squad was basically doing the same as us, hardening the compound they took over, and conducting site-sensitive exploitation. This is when we collected everything possible that could have links to tangible, reliable intelligence that can be used on the field of battle. With this phase being concluded, MEB OBJ 2 was secured and held. The assault element was also raiding the bazaar in search of food, running C-wire around the buildings we were going firm in and placing Claymore mines. They also called the remainder of my machine guns to their position because they were beginning to build machine gun positions up on the roofs and setting designated marksman and sniper hides. I remember being split from Herby at this point. He took the guns and checked in with LT and I patrolled back to the Alamo. It was only about a 25- to 30-minute patrol of less than a click or so depending on which route you took. I always found peace when I was walking on patrol. It was quiet, I had a million things running wild through my brain, and nothing all at the same time. Once we got back from dropping off the guns to LT, I checked back in with staff sergeant.

At some point during the sunlight hours Wundi had disappeared to find food. The first night there was a rooster that would crow at all hours. Wundi came back a few minutes later riding a small donkey. He rode him right into the compound and into the now open-roofed corral where we had slept the night before. It was almost shocking as this little man just trotted in on the back of a donkey like it was no big deal. He always made me laugh because he also was the toughest-looking she-man in the world, meaning he wore face paint into battle, but it wasn't in the way you would imagine. His was put on like makeup, and he wore eyeliner as well. I couldn't stop laughing about it for a long time.

I took some time that day to just observe and write in my notebook some of the things that I recognized about this experience compared to my past ones. I noticed that the fuckery is turned way down when you're fighting daily. Meaning, in the past, commands would seem to come up with new ways to fuck with junior Marines every other day and then execute whatever those plans were. When your company commander and company first sergeant are having to discharge their own weapons, they seem to care less about small issues. Something to think about, future leaders: just because you may not be in a fight, your men are every day. Imagine you were in my command's position and you may stay humble enough not to ruin the "warfighter experience" for your men.

Over the radio I heard the LT's deep voice break the net and request to speak to 2Bravo. The hook was picked up and the two conversed about the night's upcoming air drop and expectations for the following morning. It was like when SSgt. would pass the word to the platoon out by the rifle wash racks in the courtyard at Lejeune. The nightly word was passed and God willing, nothing else would have to be communicated until morning.

With the sun almost gone, we prepared our berthing for dark and tightened up the gear in the courtyard. The Marines raised the canopy to the corral, and the team leaders were checking weapons and gear for a sight count, meaning they physically put their eyes on the piece of gear they were checking. Next, I gathered the teams and selected Marines to aid in the water and food resupply if needed later. It was pretty much all the boots that wouldn't be on post, myself, and the ANA attachments. With the last orders given and received, I said my prayers quietly to myself, climbing into the corral to catch some sleep. It almost seemed like when we would be back on Lejeune at the end of the day following a hard training evolution, everyone would tighten up their gear and align the packs to the right, get the squad sight counts confirmed and hit the smoke pit for some decompression time. We literally did just the same things in country. No matter how tired I was, I always found time at the end of my day to hit the smoke pit and blow off some steam with the Marines. It was almost an unwritten rule that the smoke pit was where you could be real. Like a barber shop, you can talk amongst the others there and kind of gripe and vent a bit. Occasionally you would have a grouch like Gunny Mack yell at you in passing, but mostly people just listened and tried to feed one another gossip from the LCpl. underground.

We called it the LCpl. underground because no one ever knew where the information originated. It was spot-on when it came down to accuracy, too. The smoke pit in the early going happened to be wherever the fuck you were when you wanted to smoke just this side of being on post at night. The fact that our platoon sergeant smoked cowboy killers like that of a freight train helped in this department. Other units with nonsmoking leadership wouldn't have the same opportunities. At night it was okay to smoke but you needed to be indoors, no post or rooftop smoking for sure. Everyone cherished the privilege and ability to smoke so there were few times when Marines broke the rules; not to mention that we were actively engaged all day and some into the evening, and no one wanted to test the sniper's aim or will. Being that the canopy happened to be the sleeping area, the smoking took place there on this evening. It was short-lived as we were all exhausted and needing sleep. I laid my head down on Grime's thigh using his leg and my hoodie as a pillow and closed my eyes. He was on the resupply working party, so I would know where to find him when it was time to go.

"Wake up!" I told Grimes, as I turned off my watch alarm that woke me. I couldn't stand the rashes from wearing it on my wrist, so I attached it to my front plate just above my grenades. I felt like I'd shut my eyes for all of fifteen seconds or so, but it had been four hours. I always woke up instantly and violently when I was in country. It was like my subconscious was trying to wake me out of the fear of dying. I would always snap open and combat the chalky eyes that became the norm in the sandbox; trying to regain my grip on reality. Hypervigilance is what they call it. Some of it was from trippy dreams you would have from taking the Malaria-prevention cancer pills. They always made me have dreams of falling. We both started to move, and the word passed that the birds were inbound with the resupply. Every man on the working party or otherwise began to stir at the thought of getting some fresh chow and water. The little wins were about to be paid out in full. As we gathered around in the courtyard 2B was in COMMS with the birds trying to coordinate the drop...

WRIGHT: "Roger Sir, bring it right outside the southeast wall if possible."

CHOWwaggon: "Roger 2B, southeast wall, I see your mark. Inbound..."

SSgt. Wright was always a boss when calling in for air support, and in this moment everything seemed okay. The shots opened up on the birds from our south, down where toward Sadiqu put all the reinforcements down the day prior.

I grunted in the darkness as I knelt to hold security on the water pallet and scanned the southeast sector where the MG and rockets fired from. They seemed to be a solid distance away from us, but they peppered the choppers enough for them to force drop our water from altitude and wave off Dash 2 completely. Dash 2 had our chow resupply pallet. Thank God, I thought to myself: "Thank God nobody got shot down. That would have turned into a shitshow real fast, out there trying to save some army pilots when all of Marjah opens up on us with the first rays of sun."

I smiled and slid my grizzly wintergreen out of my shoulder pocket on my FROGG cammie top. I began to pack the can, tap... tap... tap...my index figure would thump the outer rim of the can and leave a bit of a sting each time, as it was still bitter cold. With the can packed tight I popped the top and raised it to my nose. It would wake you up in a hurry. My mouth salivated and it made me think of Pavlov's dogs, only my dinner bell was the packing of the can. My thumb and index finger on my right hand were already stained from the dip, I noticed. My wife used to hate that, and to be honest I wasn't a fan either but in the given situation it amused me and made me see her face again. I carved off the

76

perfect-sized dip for the mission at hand and quickly inserted it into its "pocket pouch" in the bottom right of my jaw, which after 10 years of dipping, was the perfect pocket. Rolling it into place with my tongue, feeling the instant burning sensation as the tiny shards of fiberglass shred my gums and dumped the poison I loved so much into my veins. I packed and then squeezed my cheeks tight to draw out some juice and spit. I always tried to do that immediately, so I could get rid of any loose specks of dip or leaves on my tongue. With the burn in full effect due to the volume of dip I was consuming, my eyes watered and the goosebumps came up my lower back with the 35-degree air. We were 150 meters or so out from the Alamo in the wide-open desert. I waited on the air to settle and the calm to approach, and proceeded to the pallet. Everything was soaking wet. The bird had to drop the pallet from too high and a bunch of the bottles exploded. I remember looking up when the bird started to take fire and thinking, "Holy shit, we're sleeping in the same field as these motherfuckers."

We didn't have an infinite supply of personnel, but what we did have was on the detail. Some held security and some carried ponchos and poncho liners of bottled water from the field back to the Alamo. 2B and I would take turns going out for loads and bringing them back, as well as each of my team leaders. We needed to get everything we possibly could back to the Alamo before sunlight. Though we weren't directly engaged, it was much more dangerous than moving at night. At some point it was my turn to take a patrol out and we ended up cleaning house as far as water was concerned. Wundi had the donkey, now dubbed KBAR, saddled up with a hauling rig, and we could load four full poncho liners of water on this poor animal. Wundi ended up cleaning the rest of what was left up with KBAR and no daylight water rescue was necessary.

Now the Alamo had somewhere around 10K bottles of water piled up like a pyramid in the courtyard. It was a lot of water. A pile of fresh bottled water had never looked this good in my entire life. However, there would be no reason to continue with the no-shave order. I was cool with this because my neck was getting to the super scratchy point by now where it starts causing the little neck rash, so I was like fuck it, let's shave. We started to get things organized by sunup and had our orders for the remainder of the day. We were to gather and transport all water possible from the Alamo to the BP. As soon as all the water was evacuated from the Alamo, we too would break down and move to the BP which to this point in time had no name and consisted of only hand-held defenses. When I arrived at the entryway on the first trip to the BP, I was greeted by a working party from the other squads to take the water from my men and move it to the holding area. Herby jumped down from a pylon and sparked two Newport cigarettes, handing one to me.

"Yo man, I got you and your boys a surprise over here in the other berthing. Come on." I followed and gathered my guys behind; we went into the berthing where the machine-gunners were as well as Hinde and his entire squad. I had the guys sit and drop Kevlars. They began to see some of the other guys from the platoon that they otherwise hadn't seen for a few days. I started to see hope and life breathe back into them, especially when Herby walked up with a giant wooden bowl of some sort and said, "This is for you and your boys, enjoy!" With a freshly lit Newport hanging out of his mouth and rocking a green USMC hoodie and a black beanie, he retrieved his Newports from his pocket and opened the pack and held it out. I grabbed one and sparked it up. To this day I am not sure what all was in the food, but we hadn't eaten in two days anyway and were running low on juice. It was an amazing concoction of eggs, chicken, potatoes and rice found on the ground throughout the bazaar. They also treated us to some imitation Debbie snack cakes they found in one store for dessert. It was truly the best meal I thought I had ever tasted, and maybe the best one I ever would taste.

The entire squad had more than enough to fill their cup and answer the long calls that their guts had been making for some time. Again, I think it is important to note that not only were these young men fighting a war, but they had been doing it literally with little to no food for multiple days now. The fact that you were hungry as a grown human and had no way to resolve the issue was taxing to one's brain alone. Now you are 18-22 and running and gunning every day for multiple days with no food. Just think about how you may feel. I know I felt weak in those couple of days. I noticed fatigue in my men as well. It was not odd to catch the lance corporals circled up around a warming fire just leaning on one another and staring off into space. This was from day fucking two.

When the squads converged for something or another, be it a mission like a water run or later for morale or reinforcements in a fight, it was always like a mini-reunion full of daps and hugs around the board. It was the beginning to the Brotherhood of Warriors. I had known of this term but many I feel threw it around loosely. You don't get that brotherhood from happy times together at the club, you don't automatically have that brotherhood bond because you share a unit designator. As my men found out, the only way there was to find out was by living it; you earned the complete respect and trust from your comrades when things were not good, when things went horribly wrong and people were written about and medals earned. When you trusted someone so much that you literally put your life in their hands, and vice versa. I think the first time I saw Grimes, Hanson, Knuckles and Merry, all lance corporals, all first deployment Marines, all best friends, from multiple different squads meeting up and hugging for the first time, was shortly after the breakfast meal. I watched as they embraced one another as brothers, forehead to forehead, 100 lbs. of gear and weapons dangling from their kits, one grabbing the other by the back of the head in embrace. Grown men who have been to and were in the middle of the ultimate arena, giving to each other everything they had every single moment of every single day, until death. That was where we began to grow the brotherhood, and through the next eight months would fine-tune it. It was one of the moments that seemed to slow down for me as if I watched it in slow motion. I wrote in my notebook that the Marines' embrace of one another was a chemistry and emotion like I had never seen or experienced in my life. We hadn't lost anyone since Vuocolo and we received word he was doing well and would be remaining up at the HQ for a bit longer. Not knowing what that meant as far as getting my best saw gunner back, I made the necessary permanent changes to the squad.

After a much-needed rest at the BP I told the TLs to roll it up and prepare to head back for more water. As we departed, I grabbed another smoke from Herby and lit it as I counted my boys out of friendly lines. We patrolled back through the bazaar and across the land bridge to the Alamo. Some of the Marines made fast "snatch and grabs" in the bazaar for candy and smokes. The bazaar and surrounding area were completely abandoned when the fighting began. By now things were beginning to rot where they laid. And of course, there was the ever-foul smell of "The Big One" that was ripening by the hour. The sorry bastard lay between the Alamo and the BP. The smells of the battlefield aren't always bad, but to this point in time they were. And it wouldn't be any better anytime soon. That's another sense that was in full alert mode. Even now, 10 years later, certain smells can take me right back to Marjah.

Back from the patrol now the TLs began to run water patrols down to the BP without me. I had run my feet to the limit and needed to take a few minutes to air out and doctor them up. Doc Fowler checked on me and said they looked bad. He recommended that I air them out and put them in the sun for a while before lacing back up. I heeded his advice and headed for the radio room. I notified the boys what I'd be doing and began the process of removing my boots and socks. When I removed my boots, it was like I felt my skin instantly begin to swell up and push out. I had my boots laced way too tight for way too long and had clearly neglected myself. As I peeled off my socks, I thought back to the 22-mile hike and what my feet looked like then. I remembered cursing the command for the "tug of war" contest after the hike and swore that they were just out to injure Marines. Now my feet were in rough shape, but not as rough as then. Not as rough as the hike. I was instantly grateful for the hike experience and smiled to a grimace as I put my socks down and cleaned my feet. The command had given us all collectively a worse foot condition to compare to with the hike. Now I saw the bigger picture. We all carried socks and foot-cleaning gear on our person, so I began there. The sun alone felt borderline orgasmic to my feet. It's like the Vitamin D is exactly what they needed to heal, and I could feel them heal. It was amazing. It was 16 February and it was the first time I had my boots off for more than 10 consecutive minutes since we woke up the morning of the 13th. I laid on my back with the hook attached to my Kevlar, I had my feet propped up on the backs of my boots and my plate carrier beside me. I "flicked my Bic" on a Newport and took in a long drag. I had positioned myself in the shade enough to see the silver-grey smoke dance and twirl in the space where the sun breaks the shadow. As I laid there in the sand observing all the different ways to blow smoke into the sky, I thought about how far I might make it through this whole invasion. I was doing well thus far but had already had so many close calls that it wasn't funny. I think we were all just kind of waiting for it to happen. That's when I really decided that it no longer mattered. I wasn't going to make it out anyway, so I needed to take advantage of the time I was given to make the best possible choices. To give everyone the best opportunity possible given the dynamics of the situation. The big picture was, we were surrounded by more fighters than were originally reported and they were much more able than were given credit for. Now there were multiple company-sized elements squeezing the city from the outside in, essentially driving the enemy right at us. Grimes walked by as his post cycle had just ended. He walked up to me laying there and said something along the lines of, "We going to make it out of here, Sergeant?" I always replied with, "You want the truth or the lie?" He always said, "Lie to me, Sergeant." So, I would lie to him and tell him, "Of course we will make it out of here." I told my Marines when I first met them that I was a straight-shooter and would never lie to them, unless they wanted me to.

We hadn't taken direct contact at our position thus far today and it was beginning to feel odd to me. The paranoia was setting in and I could no longer lay around. Every time I heard a firefight in the distance, I became drawn to scan the area to ensure we couldn't help in some way. I was thirsty for more combat and didn't even know it. The battlefield teased us all day with no direct contact, nightfall was approaching and we had only moved three-quarters of the water. There were several patrols still scheduled to run throughout the evening hours and we should be in good shape to make an entire move in the morning. Why we were moving the water was because the other squads were busy down at the BP clearing several IEDs off the area as well as several hoax IEDs in the same areas.

I knew that when talking to the LT and the other squad leaders there were like seven or eight IEDs emplaced near the MG bunkers. The fact that we had EOD as a direct asset was amazing. The ordnance was all gathered and blown in place by the techs sometime later. I say having them as a direct asset is amazing because I have been in situations in Iraq and later in the deployment in Afghanistan where I held an IED cordon with a squad for over 24 hours. It's not fun for anyone when that happens. Marines get complacent quickly when they feel as though there is someone more important than themselves, or if they feel they are being blown off by the top. I remember being in that mindset in Iraq on a few occasions.

The little gas station that the boys had captured was nice once it was cleaned up. We owned the station house and the compound across the street. We controlled the entry into and out of the main heart of northern Marjah on Route 608. It became a permanent OP for the deployment.

Word was coming in that we would have some ground assets from Lima Company opening the GLOC in the coming day or so. We were going to receive our main bags and all the mail so far that had come. This became the ever-changing unicorn prize that we never wanted to come true for us. I am certain now they did things like this as a PSYOPS way of pissing us off good before a fight. We all bedded down with the sun as we did not know what to expect in Marjah at any given point in time. You slept when they slept, basically; a rule I came to use later in life as I started becoming a father of infants.

Not knowing what the morning would have in store I tried to game it in my head as I cleaned my weapon, playing the "if this, then that" game with myself. I had two Marines on post as the boys broke down to sleep. I would always try to stay awake if I had guys up or out. I managed this by going to the radio room and listening to the battalion and company main nets. I would listen for friendly SITREPS and for my buddies' voices. On this night I told the guys to wake me for the final hour of radio watch. It was what I liked to do sometimes to get a head start on the morning. When I was woken, it was by LCpl. Wetzel, my point man. He said it was time to get up and that I had watch in 15 minutes. I got up and laced up, took my toothbrush off my chest rig, scrubbed my teeth, took a piss and properly relieved him of his watch. I remember the chatter on the main nets was extra that morning. It was somewhere around 4 a.m. when I took post and somewhere around 420 a.m. when the confused rooster began to crow. He crowed every 10 minutes or so. I hated him with a burning passion. As I was listening to 1st Platoon prepping to leave their BP for the HQ building back in Shinnywal for more batteries, they sounded cold and tired. Wundi popped his head in the radio room and said he was going to kill the rooster, motioning with his thumb across his neck. I winked at him and nodded my head.

I continued to hear the rooster for a bit, but mostly just forgot about the whole situation as I was listening to the nets for more info. I could catch Lt. Neff on my black gear occasionally, but it was mostly broken and unreadable. They were headed back before first light to the HQ to swap out batteries and get the new fill for the next week on his green gear. He had an escort by Marines from the quartering party, but I wasn't sure if they were mine or not. Suddenly, Wundi popped his head into the compound and said, "Sgt. Rrrogers," sort of rolling his tongue. He reached his hands out to me with a bowl of rice and greasy chicken. He had really found the rooster, and now we were enjoying some of Marjah's finest cock bird. I finished what I could and passed the leftovers to the guys on post outside. The longer I listened, the closer to sunrise we approached. It was exactly like back at home in the early fall, deer hunting in the early morning. Just before the sun breaks the horizon everything becomes very still, and the temperature seems to reach its coldest point. I felt the same in this moment getting an uncomfortable feeling as the first rays of sun broke the desert sky. Lt. Neff and his squad leader Sgt. Laney were now en route back to the CP and coming across the open steppe where Sadiqu had wasted the enemy with the 240 MG from the kneeling. The sun was warm, but I could still see my breath and still had my thin black beanie on my head as I made my way around, getting everyone moving again and ready to make the last of the water runs. We were about 900 meters or so north of 1st Platoon now as they were moving backward to get batteries.

Shortly after sunrise, the air began to crackle to our south where 3rd was located. I laced up and got my gear close by. I had a feeling that things were going sideways from the frantic sounds of broken transmissions coming through the XTS black gear. I couldn't make out much, but we did notice that the enemy fire was going ballistic. It sounded like multiple different machine guns and possibly RPGs depending on who was firing them. Maybe Neff had ANA with rockets too, I thought.

Over the black gear there were calls from 3rd that they had men down and they had no encrypted comms to call in support assets with. Knowing that I had Marines with that unit, and knowing we were the closest element capable to reach them with enough combat power to aid in the relief, I yelled over to SSgt. Wright that I was going for them. He told me to hang on a minute as he needed to get clearance from LT. I laced up and grabbed Knuckles, Charette, Sadiqu and "Earmuffs," our ANA RPG gunner. We called him Earmuffs because he always wore these tri-colored camo earmuffs no matter the temperature. I told SSgt. I was going to push, and he instructed me to hold on. The LT was not happy about it but having my guys in a fight with no resources was too much for me. I grabbed the radio and asked SSgt. if he was coming with me or charging me. He wasn't happy either, but he said, "I'll bring up the rear." I nodded and pushed to the southeast wall near Grimes's post. I gave him a red star cluster and told him if they started getting attacked to pop it and hold for reinforcements; we were going to help 3rd. Over the radio the crackling transmission sounded like there were multiple Marines down now, one of them KIA. This was bad, I thought. I pushed out the southeast exit in a sprint. LCpl. Wetzel accompanied me as we echeloned out in pairs. We ran the entire way, the gunfire getting louder and louder as we closed. I was in great shape, but my lungs burned as we ran in the cold air. Soon we were coming up to the northeast edge of the mass of buildings I believed 3rd Platoon was located. We were about 300 yards out now when we stopped for a break to try to contact 3rd. We needed a connecting file to guide us through the area as we didn't know where the enemy was even firing from, and we needed to wait for the rest of our element to close the gap, most of whom were now slowed to a walk. Only seconds had gone by and the connecting file popped out the back of a compound to the south and waved us in. SSgt. Wright was still way behind but we left Marines to walk them in, and we had good squad communications now. If he was turned around, we would have eyes on him anyway and he had multiple ANA and a Marine or two with him.

When I walked into the courtyard for the first time, I saw an entire platoon gazing around and staring off into space. My buddy from 3/2, Timmy Smith, was shot in the initial contact and it tore the entire top of his forearm off. I remember coming into compound and seeing him and the officer Lt. Neff completely green. Physically they were in a bit of shock and they literally looked green in the face. A few Marines from 3rd were on post, but not acting effectively. They were all just chilling, not returning fire on the enemy or taking any proactive measures. I grabbed my first few Marines close by and started to move through the interconnected compounds. I placed LCpl. Knuckles with his SAW on the northeast corner just outside the courtyard wall watching our six. I then dropped over a compound and set up a machine gun position there with Sadiqu by knocking a portion of the mud wall out with the buttstocks of the weapons. He set in and started to fire on one confirmed enemy position, instantly achieving hits, shutting the enemy gun down. Next, I went back to the firm site and observed the rest of Sgt. Laney's guys begin to come back to life. He too was now setting in guns and taking the fight back to the enemy. SSgt. Wright was now coordinating the link-up with air to evacuate our dead and wounded. He was always the calmest person on the battlefield, I tried to emulate that.

I ran back to the compound to pay my respects to PFC Eric Currier who was hit with bullets from a machine gun burst. He was laying on a big pile of feed and fertilizer covered up with someone's poncho liner. I remember thinking about how the faces of the dead always seemed so at peace. Currier was one of the new guys that was picked up from SOI and checked in while we were on pre-deployment leave. I knelt beside him and pulled the poncho liner off his body. He looked at peace, he looked like a hero. He was in good shape for number of times he'd been hit. I said a short prayer, thanking him for his sacrifice and apologizing that he had been called up so soon. I covered him back up and proceeded out the courtyard and back to work.

That is all the goodbye that we are given. Even when it is someone like your best friend, there is never ample time to say goodbye when people are dying. Then they end up being flown out of zone and buried within a short time and you are still in a mud hut wondering how the funeral must have gone. You wonder if anyone told the best parts about him, and if he was as good as you are choosing to remember him. I didn't know this kid well, but he was my brother, he fell on the same field, shed his blood in the same sand.

When I walked out, we needed to ramp up the east side as we were really being hit hard. I reported to the northeast to check on Knucks and the backside. He was tucked much further into the door than I had placed him. As I walked up, I asked why that was. He responded, "There is a really good sniper out there, Sergeant." I had not seen much activity from snipers yet, so I arrogantly stepped out from the door to get my bearing and look. I realized within about the first half-second that this was a mistake, as a 7.62 mm round struck beside my head by about six inches or so, striking the door frame made of mud and splintering little mud pieces into my right cheek and neck. I bolted back into the door laughing and agreeing instantly with Knucks, that the sniper was a good shot. He was elevated almost 100 feet up in a Russian-built radio tower that sat in the cemetery upon a hill overlooking the area where our bazaar was, which was directly north of our new position by the bazaar about 800 meters away. It was reported that the sniper was a hired Chechen gun, but that was secondhand information. They were notorious for having some of the best snipers. They typically were using 7.62 mm long guns but occasionally they would have some serious firepower. I'm not sure who called the air in on this guy, but it came in the form of a Cobra and knocked the sniper from his perch easily. The GAL is a bad piece of machinery.

Back to the fight, I left Knuckles and moved to an area where the resistance was really picking up. I remember trying to ID the enemy at one point in time. They would fire at anything they saw come out in the open. I made a run or two and so did SSgt. Wright, ultimately drawing the enemy to fire so that we could hit him hard. I had a polar-shift mission from me to the enemy spun up and I called it out as Wright echoed it back to me and into the radio. We called it in "danger close" as the enemy compound was only 150 meters out and I lit a smoke. As the shots were sent into the air they called "shot over" into the radio. "Shot out," Wright replied, and I shouted for everyone to get small. I took a long drag of my Newport and looked down at the G-Shock watch attached to my rig above my grenades. "Three seconds," I said to myself and I popped up to peer over the wall to observe the round impact. I made a small adjustment and called out "fire" for effect. Again, Wright repeated me into the PRC-117 and again the gun crew called out the shot. This time it was several shots as we were firing for effect on the confirmed target. The most brilliant display of firepower rained down on the enemy compound with flashes of light and some of the most earth-moving booms I had ever heard. By the time the rounds were completed the enemy was no longer running shit. Makes one wonder, what would have happened if the batteries never died and Lt. Neff could have instantly been able to make it rain; would they have needed us? I think the lesson in this story is to always top off on batteries when you can and when it is safe to do so; also when you're traveling in the daytime, in a hot zone, it is best to get big dispersion and have on-call targets to reference to your gun crews. Even when you think you're okay, you're not. Always assume you will be hit today, in an hour, right now...

We were able to mitigate that threat well as the fighters showed zero resistance after being blown up. The mission was a big success for the gun crew and us. It was my first real-world kills with 81s and I'm pretty sure the crew's first as well. Once the choppers had come and evacuated the dead and wounded, we were still in the shit with the Taliban on the ground. We fought for a period of almost five hours that day before returning to the Alamo at almost dark, as one or two pop-shots came at us per minute, just harassing us as we broke back. I remember SSgt. Wright setting up and waiting for one of them to fire again and try to move. He was waiting for it and fired back when the fighter fired at us. Wright dumped a magazine of well-aimed shots to no avail. But they did stop harassing us. We made it back to the Alamo a completely different unit than we had started the morning as. Now we had a lost man and now the feelings were all a bit different.

To see a friendly down is one thing, but to see a Marine down hard, especially one that is on the same field of battle you are, to see the US MARINES on the chest as you load them onto a bird, is just not good. It does something to your confidence. When I saw Currier on the feed bags, I was okay, but Wetzel my point man had temporarily lost his shit. When he did, SSgt. Wright told him to shape up. He started getting emotional and crying; maybe it was his mortality being humbled, maybe he just needed to vent it out after four or five days, or maybe it was because he was pissed. Whatever the situation, it was handled poorly, as everyone was completely stressed to the max. Wright yoked him up through all the crying and slammed him up against the wall. I intervened and told Wright that "he was my Marine and I would handle it from here but thank you." With the rounds still cracking he went back to the fight and I took care of Wetzel. I am not sure what happened during the work-up before I came to the platoon, but Wetzel was not liked much by SSgt. Wright.

Multiple times throughout our push I had to cover down on the kid for fear of him being fucked with. I told him that if he didn't want anyone else to die then he needed to be able to utilize his RCO optic on his weapon, and that he could only do that if he didn't have tears in his eyes while trying to engage. He seemed to shore up rather quickly and we left it at that.

Sometimes max violence is the way in a combat zone, and sometimes it's not. Wetzel was a great Marine and an amazing point man. He just seemed to get overloaded that day with the sights and smells and sounds of death and war. The patrol back was close to sundown as we had been fighting most of the day. With the 3rd Platoon now clear to make the trip the rest of the way to the HQ, we broke off and departed for the Alamo. When we left, Lt. Neff grabbed me and shook my hand. He thanked me for coming for them and said he wouldn't forget about it. He was in better shape now and the color had returned to his face. He and Laney had a grasp on things and were no longer being shot at. I tipped my Kevlar to Sgt. Laney and fired up a Newport. I took a long drag in and called over the black gear for the boys to roll it up. We departed the dilapidated Shinnywal for the Alamo. I was completely out of water from where I let Timbo get my hose shortly after arriving on scene. He downed my entire two-liter camelback and I was left to fight for the next several hours on no water. I did not make this mistake again in the future. The guys getting on the bird back to Leatherneck were going to be having hot nurses and ice cream cakes before fucking sundown and you're going to be in the suck here, still playing with guns. Give them a sip and send them on their way.

I was prepared to get my ass chewed by the LT when I returned from the fight that day, but it never came. I didn't really see him as he was at the firm station and I was stuck at the Alamo. The next morning would be upon us fast, so we started the post cycle and bedded everyone down for the evening. After passing the word, I took Wetzel to the side and spoke to him man to man about the events of the day. He understood the severity of the consequences for his emotional fit under fire, and I was aware that everyone was shaken at that point and it was bound to happen to someone. Death and killing are just not natural to the human psyche. I told him I understood what he was thinking, and that it's not easy, to get some rest and forget the day.

Tomorrow we would be making the permanent move to the BP and reuniting with our other comrades. We would be living with the machine guns and 1st Squad. I hadn't seen Herby or Scotty in a few firefights, so I made a morale trip with the first trip out with water in the morning. We would do this for each other from time to time throughout the deployment, sometimes for birthdays, sometimes just to check on each other. This is the refinement of the brotherhood. It's not an obligation; it's a want and a need to check on your men, your brothers.

I wasn't greeted with the bowl of eggs like the day before, but I did meet up with the other two legs of the tripod to share some stories from the past 24 hours and burn down a few American smokes. I climbed up on the new MG post up on top of the station house that JT and LT were taking refuge in. You could see for a long way. I remember sitting up there burning a Newport just staring into the abyss of sand and broken dreams. I thought about how Currier's family would think of all of this. To be sure, they were hesitant sending their son to the Marines especially during wartime. But this kid gave his life for his country in the first week of being in zone, less than two months after graduating the School of Infantry. These people no more than got to update photo albums with boot camp blues photos before it was over. I to this day don't know how Gold Star families remain as thankful and caring as they do. It's surely a daunting task that I pray I never experience. I thanked God that I was not a father; my daydream once vivid was now breaking up and melting back to reality, as my middle finger and index began to burn where I was holding the smoke. I had smoked it down to the filter. With a quick snap and flick of the middle digit the cherry flew off the filter and down into the sand, leaving a twirling tail of smoke all the way to the ground. The word came in that the first sergeant and CO would be making their way down to us shortly, probably as a morale booster and mail drop. Not wanting to be around for that I told the TLs to roll it up and prep to depart for the Alamo.

With daps and hugs out of the way we laced up and hit the road. We were stoked to get back to the Alamo, so we could make the permanent move down with all our gear. This meant we could start some sort of routine and not have to "live out of bags," as they say, though we were living out of bags. It's the difference between staying at your brother's house for a holiday and operating your entire five-person family out of suitcases, versus renting the Airbnb for less money and everyone having their own nice little place away from home. It's just better for everyone. To this point in time, I felt solid as a squad. We had a few hiccups so far, but everyone was firing on all cylinders when it counted and for that I was thankful.

Getting back and finding the Marines burning the remaining bottles of water was almost comical. Who told you to burn water bottles? SSgt. Wright told the Marines to cut, empty, and burn everything that was left. It wasn't much, but we had all been topped off already and the other platoons had already made trips to us for resupply. With everyone topped off we burned the bottle trash and buried the bulky stuff in the sand. We signed off with the Alamo and she became nothing more than a mud hut once more, now only remembered in the dusty scribbles of the United States Marines. We left the Alamo and patrolled to the new refuge where we would live for the unforeseeable future, or at least until Lima Company opened the GLOC. Once this happened, we could get the engineers in here to begin construction of a forward operating base (FOB).

608 Picket/Camp Construction/LCpl. Hanson

It was the morning of 18[th.] We were all back together again. Second Platoon and all attachments were now consolidated and hardening our position in the expectation of a counterattack by the Taliban. Our assumption was that they would hit us with everything that they had to stop our invasion and then they would be humbled and disappear. These fighters were tough, though. They were tough, and they were dedicated. They also had the lack of drug use restrictions and rules of engagement to abide by, so they were basically invincible in their own eyes, which can work in your favor big time. They were also using women and children as human shields the past few days, driving a burning hatred for the Taliban and any who supported them.

We continuously kicked out security patrols around the clock and tightened up our defenses and the days became long. The fighting is the cherry on top of a workup and complete deployment; sometimes complete campaigns of waiting in absolute boredom watching sand not grow, becoming almost immune to the elements, but not really. But let's be honest, going from 30-degree cold to 120-degree heat in three months is rough on the psyche. The lack of food and knowledge of when you would eat again. The uncertainty in almost every single need that you have. When your needs are basic, I found it easier to cope with horrible shit. When your needs are met it's easier to become more self-aware and focus your attention on things that otherwise did not ever present a problem before. For us in Marjah this was a good thing. You could do some horrible shit and put up with some horrible shit when you're living in a mud hut and scrounging for food on the daily, not knowing if your day is today or tomorrow.

Before too long the distant sound of a convoy was heard moving in. It was Lima Company opening up the GLOC to us a week into the push. We were in desperate need of our main packs that were palletized and set to be transported to us when the GLOC finally opened. As Lima Company rolled up and through the position, they made mention of having IEDs everywhere and they were hit with multiple complex ambushes that were initiated by EFP (explosively formed penetrator) and command detonated IEDs. Our higher-ups and intel nodes exchanged information and they moved on.

They would be pushing further to the north and establishing their own COP. In the following days we would be sent some engineers to build the battalion's Forward Operating Base (FOB). I had been there all of a few hours to this point and LT had a mission for my squad. We were to patrol out the west end of the bazaar and up to the radio tower where the Chechen sniper had been perched the few days prior. The base of the radio tower was all concrete and had a locked double door. They had a small command building the base as well as some electronic huts of all reinforced concrete. The LT wanted us to have the position because it directly overlooked our position. We could have the enemy getting back into the tower with a sniper rifle, or, God forbid, rockets or a machine gun. I witnessed a machine gun on multiple occasions command authority on the battlefield, leveraging multiple squads at one time.

One well-trained gunner or sniper can wreak havoc on an Area of Operation (AO), especially when your rules of engagement are known by the enemy and you have semi-ruined your long-range indirect fire capabilities with the rogue HIMARS attack. I had visited it in my thoughts now frequently, whether they were good or bad, bad or unlucky, unlucky or deserving. I suppose when it came to the raw emotion, I felt that it was better them than my men or myself. I left it at that, kind of making them the enemy with no second thoughts about it. The feelings were helpful and served a purpose at the time. I would always tell my men what I had been told by my superiors: "You will have the rest of your life to think about this shit. Right now you need to stay clear-minded." The quote couldn't be truer, and to be honest, who knew if we would get out anyway? We all adopted that line of thinking, I think. I know that I did.

After I received the FRAGO from the LT I went back to my berthing area and rounded up the guys. It was early afternoon on February 18th as Squad was prepping to push out of friendly lines yet again. I talked to the guys and we packed light day packs and overnight kits. We weren't to be out very long as JT's squad would be relieving us the following day. We needed to work up to the tower and clear it out. Following the clear we needed to hold it overnight, and then retain control of the tower and hill. It was the most dominating high ground and high key terrain feature in the area of operation. Knowing that nobody else had gone up there yet, I knew it was possible that the enemy may be present. I briefed the squad that we would be moving up at night and to use the cover of darkness to make the movement, and we would be clearing and holding overnight. I would roll with the first team on the clear, and if necessary, we would use the quarter stick of TNT hooked up to a nice little EOD blasting cap that SSgt. Stinard rigged up for us to pop locked doors with. He was one of our attached EOD techs. The boys all broke out to rest and refit for the mission and they scattered about the courtyard. At this point I had Knuckles, Grimes and Mickiewicz sick with dysentery, throwing up and shitting themselves. The little sore on Mickiewicz's leg was also in bad shape. It was clearly infected from what I could tell but I wanted Doc H. to give it a look as well. He stayed in JT's berthing across the street in the gas station with LT. I wasn't sure Mack should go up to the tower with us or not. I called Doc Fowler over to look at his leg and do a general wellness check on my sick guys, as he was at my berthing.

Most of the Marines were in the hut and were called out to be looked at. Nobody looked one hundred percent, but all in all not too bad. We had some cold legs and some dysentery but other than that we were good until Fowler checked Mackie's leg out. Initially he wanted to medevac him. He told me it looked really infected and that if he indeed had an infection in these conditions it could get bad fast. I grabbed my black gear off my plate carrier (PC) and tried to raise Doc H. on the hook. I advised him on my location and asked if he could come take a look at Mackie. When he showed up a few minutes later SSgt. was with him, as usual hobbling his barrel-chested frame of about 6 foot 2 around like he's done this shit the past 14 years. When we looked at Mackie, he was projectile vomiting to the side of the bucket he was washing his FROG top in. He had puked on his shirt and wanted it to smell better before we stepped in to do whatever was next. I remember feeling so bad for him. He was already in a shitty situation; being sick just added insult to injury. The command slapped the table on evacuating if the issue worsened. The sun was starting to drop in the sky as I left Mackie with the corpsman and walked back over to get my squad moving. I would need to notify Mackie's TL that he wouldn't be making the tower trip, and we would have to make some adjustments yet again to the teams. At this point I had lost V to the sniper and now Mackie was close due to the leg infection, but he would be back in a relatively short period of time, if he left at all. I racked my brain on what the best move was, as far as the teams that were to be arranged if that happened. It started to look like the best decision would be to collapse down to two teams run by Cpl. Charette and Cpl. Bennet; I would float between the two teams where needed and when necessary, and have Grimes run the third team.

I wasn't overly confident in Cpl. Simmering's ability to lead, but I was certain he could handle the PIG. He proved that on the first morning dropping the runner in the tree line. Grimes was proving to be a CDMF. I had heard this term one time from my dad. He was telling me a story about a boss that he had. His boss called him a CDMF one night after work, my father asked what it meant, and the man told him it stood for "can-do motherfucker." I think it was a talk about work ethic, like "message to Garcia," just find a way to get the task accomplished. He may have had a bit of a belly, but he was cool under fire and I liked that. Your number one and most important tool or weapon in a fight is your mind. You can be a crack shot and a PT stud, but if you can't compose your thoughts and clear the mind you will always be a step behind the enemy. These people literally have been at war forever. And they recruit young men at the ripe age of 11 or 12 sometimes against the families' wishes. They then put them in training camps where they learn to kill Americans according to a swayed and radicalized version of the Koran. I added that little piece to compare it to our fresh Marines in combat, who have trained for less than a year. The Taliban 20-year-old is far more experienced than the Marine 20-year-old, especially in terms of what they believe the world is. For a 20-year-old Taliban soldier, death is common and gore is welcomed. Unfortunately, the tactic of attaching a radical idealism to something as deep-seated as the people's religion was the work of an evil genius. Then you recruit them in young, maybe alter the Koran a bit, and sell them a load of bullshit guaranteeing 77 virgins in the afterlife. Bada bing, bada boom. I shook my head as I thought on the way back to the berthing.

I rounded up the TLs and informed them about Mackie and the shift in the squad that was coming should we evacuate him in the coming days. Nothing would change much for the tower mission, but it may become a bigger issue later, I told them. I told the boys we would be conducting PCCs and PCIs as soon as the sun started to fade. I wanted to be ready to move as soon as the sun was down completely. I remember it being the middle of the month but the end of the moon cycle. It was crazy dark out. I briefed the squad that we would be moving in a "ranger file" up to the compound in order to mark and bypass IEDs if necessary. We had found a bunch down by the bazaar and in between the machine gun bunkers. Spreading everyone out just runs the risk of someone finding the dead-end path to walk on, literally.

As we departed the lines, I could see my breath a bit. I called over the radio to Bennett that I was traveling with Charette up front and that I wanted his team to pull up the rear. He copied and confirmed, and we continued out the lines. I put the squad into a tactical column until we were out of the bazaar, at which point we moved into a "ranger file" with about 20 meters' dispersion between each man. We would remain in this formation until the objective rally point at the top of the hill. Once at the ORP we would consolidate and then make movement together to stack and clear the radio tower. As we walked in the brisk, still night, all one could hear was the crispy crunch of the Marines' boots as they planted firmly on the desert floor. The crunch came from the condensation left by the evening's dew which froze with the sudden drop in temp. Occasionally, you would hear a scuffle where some new boot tripped because he didn't get trained long enough on his night optic devices (NOD). When wearing them, your depth perception is thrown off considerably with the NVGs and even more so, in my opinion, with the mini-thermals. Even though we were in active combat, I still laughed every time I saw one of them bite the dust.

It was always spooky walking through the bazaar at night. There were so many places that someone could be hiding or waiting for you. Picture a bazaar as a strip mall of a bunch of smaller stores all trying to sell something. Both sides of the street have storage lockers that have roll-up doors on them, and inside may be hanging meat rotting at this point or other merchandise such as snack food, ice and knickknacks. The store owners still hadn't returned with their families from the desert. As you would guess, the bazaar was raunchy with the rotting meat. Everyone seemed to go nomadic unless they stayed to fight us. Once they returned, the bazaar would surely be cleaned up and back to normal, which I was afraid was still highly unhealthy.

Considering the circumstances, who gave a fuck anyway; this all goes back to the hierarchy of needs talked about in the last chapter. When your food needs aren't being met you will absolutely lower your standards of what is considered edible and what is not. This is the same with your living arrangements and your everyday give-a-fuck about otherwise insignificant things. I cringed a bit as the thought of being hit from a dark corner came over me. I flipped on my white light to check the area. My white light was attached to my M4 on the left-hand side of the barrel attached to a mil-spec Picatinny rail surrounding my barrel. I had my floodlight mode on for this very reason. On the other side of the light, was a PEQ-16. It had IR laser capability and different filter caps that allowed for different types of marks and communications. All these things were detailed in our signal plan, found in each operation order. As far as the PEQ-16 goes, they were our primary source of aiming and accuracy in a gunfight at night. We had zeroed the lasers just before pushing into Marjah and had not really gotten to use them for anything other than marking buildings and doors to different members of the squad at night. When I flipped on the flood light, there was nothing in the corner other than a dried-up stack of poppy stems.

I was anxious to get to the radio tower so we could get settled in. I was extremely tired as I hadn't slept well yet. Not thinking that I was going to get much sleep up here either, but one can wish. As we closed the bazaar out, I gave the hand and arm signal to close the column down into a ranger file and pick up the speed a bit. I could see the hill plainly in front of us now and the headstones and black flags and banners flying over them. We learned that the black sashes and scarves signified a Taliban member. If this was the case, it was a Taliban cemetery. Every headstone had a black sash flying from it, rippling in the desert wind.

In our final movement up to the front side of the compound which now felt much bigger than it looked from the firm base, we crept with soft feet. I held a quarter stick of dynamite and my front frag pouch on my kit in case the door was locked. I also was carrying a red star cluster in my kit, which was the signal for friendlies to come aid if we needed reinforcements. The walls were about 15 feet tall and just as thick as the mud hut walls. The inside courtyard couldn't have much room as there looked to be multiple outbuildings; the space inside the walls was not that large. I remember it was painted white and red like a cell tower back home or the big water towers painted red and white on base back at Lejeune. I remember seeing them sticking out like a sore thumb saying hello as we went across the overpass to get on base.

The assault team stacked up on the entry to the courtyard and the squeeze came forward from the rear. I was the number two man in the stack when we made entry. The door had already been unlocked so there was no need to blow it with the explosives, as badly as I wanted to. The entry was smooth, and the compounds were all empty. As soon as we had the doors closed behind us, the Marines went into action, picking up their responsibilities and getting each other up and onto the roofs, setting into a post cycle that must have been prearranged by the TLs. Bennett and Charette were outstanding when it came to having shit like that handled and out of the way so that it wasn't an issue. Like I said, it's the little wins that get you through hell. The little things like that are paramount to a successful operation.

This night was a very trying night for myself and my squad. We were sent up here to retain control of the key terrain feature and overwatch the area until further notice, seemingly an easy mission. By the time the boys were set in place and overwatch was established we started picking up traffic on the battalion net that the snipers were out in our area and needed some illumination rounds fired. About the time the radio chatter broke the silence Knuckles and Grimes began throwing up violently. I was told they were throwing up but there was nothing we could do about it. I had them rotate back down and replaced them with Bridges and Simmering. They, too, were sick. Some were shitting, and some were puking. I never contracted dysentery at this point but virtually my entire squad did. With nothing to be done about the Marines getting sick, I told them to try to stay hydrated the best they could and switch out when they were ill.

I had a very hard time staying awake that evening, like I just couldn't hold my eyes open. Bennett and I were switching on and off with the radio watch. Whoever was on radio watch was also in charge of checking on the boys' topside. Many times that night I had to be shaken awake by my guys. Mostly Bennett, and sometimes Grimes. It was a joint effort that night to remain diligent and awake as a unit. When I failed, my guys picked me up, and vice versa. At one point the loom mission for the snipers went through and we could hear the far-off boom off outgoing from the 81s, followed by the loom bursting right over our position. I immediately rolled the net and made my command aware that we were being exposed by those motherfuckers and would appreciate it being handled. The guys' topside became exposed and vulnerable until the canister fizzed out and it was dark once more, which seems like forever when you're exposed.

Especially when you're in Marjah in enemy territory, on a hill in the middle of a graveyard. We had about eight hours until daylight and we felt every one of them, between hourly wake-ups to the sound of vomit hitting the ground or loom rounds popping nearby to the smell that such vomit puts out to the chilly air that seemed at this point all but consumed by death. I know I must have fallen asleep many times that night.

"Sgt. Rogers, get up, man," Bennett said as he shook me once more. "You need to get up man, come on." I guess it was all the lack of sleep finally wearing on me or something, I just could not get with it. I must really compliment Bennett with keeping shit together for the last half of that mission because I felt like I had been drugged. When I finally came back to the earth it was daylight and the squad was moving about the compound, tightening things up. I had been out of it most of the night and now Jesse was taking control of the situation. He had the radio and the boys were cleaning the puke from the night and setting in sandbags for protection. I got my shit together and pulled myself to my feet. I had fallen asleep sitting on the concrete under a poncho liner outside the main building. I pulled my toothbrush out of my molly straps under my grenades and scrubbed the sweaters off my teeth. I washed my face and rinsed my hair out. Once I was back completely, Bennet walked over and gave me an update of things to be done and communications from LT while I was out. We would be relieved later in the afternoon and we needed to have the area ready to be turned over to JT's guys. He had the guys build posts and get the bulk of the vomit cleaned up. They did this by throwing sand on the puke piles and then using E-tools to scoop and move the clumpy sand puke-pile.

During the day I popped up to the top multiple times to get a look at everything. You could see the entire battlespace from the previous days from this vantage point and it was no wonder the sniper from days before had chosen this platform. It was perfect, I thought, as I took a long drag off a Newport. I started to scan the area around us through my RCO on top of my M4. The rifle combat optic has a four-power magnification to it giving the user a little more distance.

Just north of the cemetery down the hill a few hundred meters was a small village of interconnected compounds much like Shinnywal had looked. There were several buildings that were flying black flags outside their homes, but this wasn't enough to give hostile act or intent, and the enemy knew that. We observed the village most of the day and recorded the things we observed. All the buildings in the little village seemed to be buzzing which was rare. Some of the guys got started on some range cards and some fire-plan sketches of the posts. A fire-plan sketch is a basic sketch of everything that you see from your fighting position, labeling roads, buildings and dead space that your weapon system cannot cover. Then you also have ranges to certain key terrain features. The idea is that a completely new person could set into the fighting position and look at the card and know everything needed to defend the position properly.

Nobody was sure what was to come next. Some rumors were surfacing that the battalion wanted us to remain back for the colonel's personal element; some said we would be moving out east of the Camp Allen area in general; and some said we would never leave the location we were currently inhabiting. With the ground line open, I was confident that we would get our main packs and maybe even some mail. We still were wearing what we inserted in and hadn't had main packs or changes of clothes or sleeping bags. There was some traffic in the way of trucks and engineers throughout the day up at the radio tower, so we had some sense of hope that we would go back to some sort of surprise.

We could hear over the radio that 3rd Squad was exiting friendly lines to come up and RIP (Relief in Place) us out of the radio tower. This just means to relieve us of the post, so we can return to refit. They took much longer getting up to us because it was daylight hours and they found several IEDs that we very luckily didn't step on in the night movement to the tower. They marked and passed the IEDs to let the EOD teams come disarm or remove them. It turned out that the IED were mostly hoax IEDs and some were real but were no longer connected to power. It's hard to tell sometimes. With the danger marked, we would have a certain route to take back to the lines. The techs came out later that evening to collect and blow the ordnance in place. On the way back, they took four satchels of C4 and demoed the two MG bunkers.

Exhausted from the night and the sleepless week thus far, we rolled it up and set off from the tower to go home to the berthing inside the compound in the bazaar. We traveled back in a staggered column with big time dispersion. We were never tight front to back or side to side when the sun was out. Once back, we briefed the LT on the night's events and started to break down for chow and weapons maintenance. We didn't have anything waiting on us by way of surprise. We had been here a week with the same gear we entered with and some of the clothes were fucking wrecked.

The next 12 hours were a blur. We went back to the COP and were completely smoked as a unit. I got more sleep than the boys did up at the tower, but I was still exhausted. I stopped by the COP COC to give the mission debrief to SSgt. and LT, and then headed for the other side of the street. We ate, cleaned weapons and wracked out in our squad hut. It was completely black when the tarp door was down, as there were no windows. You could see where they cut windows out during the summer months and sealed them up during the cold season. Regardless, there was zero light getting in. We all slept well that night as we got taken care of on the post roster. There was word the following day that the GLOC was going to be opened completely and we may be visited by the command or have Lima Company rolling through our position. No one really knew anything for sure, but we tightened up the area anyway and awaited our companions. Maybe they would have fresh dip or mail, we wondered. Some guys were excited to get mail and others were just excited to receive their main packs with all their packed-up creature comforts. I personally was really missing my warming layers. Once my blood was going, I made my way across the street to see what the day had in store for me and to get a cup of MRE coffee.

React duties were all duties taking someone outside the wire, be they to pursue bad guys or conduct security patrols to ensure nobody was plotting on us.

I cannot remember the exact time, but at some point in the afternoon I was tacked up on the roof with one of the boys and we saw the trucks pushing in from a distance. It was Lima Company escorting ground engineers. They were moving slowly through the desert, stretched out several miles, it seemed, traveling from north to south toward us with a wall of sand kicking up behind them. You could hear the occasional firefight coming from the south in 1/6's area of operation AO to the south as well. Lima Company would have our packs and the engineers would build us a real COP; the big wins were coming. As close as they seemed to us, it was a long time before they finally made it. For hours, it seemed, we watched them twist and turn, navigating the plentiful canal systems, sometimes having to deploy the portable bridges designed for this exact circumstance. We would occasionally hear an IED find one of their mine-rollers that roll out in front of the trucks to protect the actual Marines and equipment from the pressure-switch IEDs. It was always unnerving when a blast would go off. You would hope it was a mine-roller and pray that everyone was okay. With explosives this heavy, a truck would be fucked if it took a direct hit, even with the 30 thousand pounds of armor. I took the last cigarette out of the pack of Newports I opened the night prior at the tower and fired it up. I crumbled up the old pack and set it on fire behind the sandbags. I took a long draw and thought about going down to the hut to get some rest. I believe in country I thought about sleeping far more than I slept. After what seemed like an eternity, Lima linked up with our company command and the next thing you know the engineers were rolling up with bulldozers to the base of the radio tower hill. They were beginning what would be our new home. The dozers had gun trucks with them, but there were also engineers in the vehicles and in the turrets behind the guns.

A while had passed with the trucks and dozers working up on the hill when a shot rang out in their direction. I don't even remember hearing the shot but the radio transmissions that followed I remember quite well. I remember LT communicating with the engineers about taking fire. The engineers were essentially requesting to fire back at someone taking shots at them. LT explained this to the other end of the radio and told them the next time they took fire to hit them with one of their truck-mounted 240s. It wasn't long after that communication that a shot followed by a 240 burst rang out. The engineer gunner had hit the would-be Taliban shooter with a burst. Being that my squad was on react, my black gear started chirping with a FRAGO from the LT. I was to go up to the site and conduct a dead check on the downed enemy and conduct a battle damage assessment or BDA. A dead check is simply that, checking to see if the person is dead or alive. The best way I found is to flick the eyes or do a sternum rub. If someone dies with their eyes open it is easy to tell if they are dead. I informed the squad and began to lace up. While on react, the squad staged their entire kits in our berthing in order to move quickly when required, much the same way that firefighters have all of the gear on standby, so they merely stand into the kit and are ready to move to the emergency. We were able to be out of friendly lines in a very short amount of time. The mission was simple, and following PCCs and PCIs, we stepped for the hill. With the area being overwatched by the gun trucks and MGs, I felt okay to move quickly through the bazaar. We blew open into a tactical column following the bazaar and made our way up to the cemetery. When I linked up with the gun-trucks they pointed me in the area where the man was shot.

The squad went into action, instantly cordoning off the compound and getting set for entry. The downed man lay just in the back side of the courtyard wall, like he was picked off his firing platform. With the compound area secure, I made my way to conduct a dead check and collect any site-sensitive material that may be around the area or on his person. I knelt beside the man, who was around 30 years old or so, with a black and white salt-and-pepper beard groomed tightly to his face. He looked better nourished than the average local. He had a grey dishdasha that came down to his mid-shins, and he wore black rubber sandals and a small hat that now lay beside him. He was hit multiple times by the burst but was surprisingly clean. His eyes were open and he had almost a peaceful look on his face, but clearly there was zero electricity in him. His eyes were greyed over with the look of death. I remember doing a soft eye tap to ensure I was correct, but for the life of me cannot remember if I closed his eyes or left them open. Regardless, nothing was on or around the man that seemed sensitive, so we let him lay and started to question the farmers who were walking up outside the compound. I wanted to know where the weapon was that this man was using. There were clearly spent shell casings on the ground where he now lay, but no weapon. The few farmers that I spoke to in the area were very hesitant to speak to us at all. One of the farmers claimed that the man was simply farming and was shot for no reason. With the aid of my interpreter I spoke to one more person, an older woman who was covered by a headdress and dishdasha from head to toe. She told me to not go down on the other side of the cemetery; that they were all bad and we wouldn't make it out of there. I couldn't really tell if she was warning me or baiting me, but I took what she said into consideration and saved it all for the debrief. With there being nothing else notable to attend to, we broke down and rolled back to the COP. The day was long and slow, but we got some needed intel on the enemy and would build the mission accordingly.

February 21st

The morning came early as we had spent most of the evening debriefing the dead check mission and building the follow-on mission. When you tell Marines not to go somewhere and do it in a condescending manner, it's taken somewhat as a double dog dare. Marines need to be cognizant of this so as to not run headstrong into an ambush. We, in this situation, measured the mission carefully and agreed that it was either investigate the probable threat and be in front of it or wait on the probable threat to hit us and hope we were ready. This was a very easy decision to make, especially because we would be staying here a while and it would be one less thing to worry about hurting us. Once the table was slapped on the mission, the squad leaders broke out to brief the guys and get bedded down. It would be my squad and Sgt. Hinde's boys.

When I woke up, the entire hut was blacked out minus one tiny hole in the tarp door that was letting this single beam of light in, which to me in that place at that time was one of the most beautiful things I had ever seen. I laid and watched the dust particles that I was breathing in all night dance in that single beam of light. I sparked a fresh Newport to find everyone not on post clustered up, spooning in the hooch in twos and threes, trying to stay comfortable and warm. I inhaled a long first draw and held the smoke in my lungs until they burned. The hot cherry now the only light in the room, I exhaled the smoke and watched it dance in the single beam. That was more realistic to me; this whole motherfucker is going to burn, I thought, starting today. I kicked and bumped the people touching me and got everyone moving. We weren't in a huge rush, but we did need to get moving so we could prep our gear and shit before stepping. I always liked to enter the battlefield with an empty stomach. I was always afraid I'd shit all over my self and be all nasty through a gunfight. It was usually the last thing I did before lacing up. I remember specifically needing an extra Nalgene bottle for the op, because mine got broken off my kit in one of the preceding fights. I asked around to my squad if there was any picked up.

With no luck I made my way across the lot to Hinde's squad area. I asked Hinde if he had an extra and he said no.

"Hear ya go Sgt. Rogers. I have an extra one."

I turned to find Lance Corporal Hanson standing there extending out his personal Nalgene bottle. He was one of Sgt. Hinde's point men. I reached out and grabbed it and said, "Thanks brother!"

"No worries Sgt. Just don't get shot, I want that back!"

I laughed and told him not to get blown up. We both laughed that unexpected laugh where you raise your eyebrows knowing it's possible. I patted him on the shoulder and walked back over to my squad area and started to prep my gear and make sure the boys were moving.

At this point in time the company command location was still back in Shinnywal where they initially set up, and where we slept the first night in Marjah. The other platoons were conducting operations much the same way we were. They too had hardened their compounds and started conducting patrolling ops.

"COC, COC, this is 2-2 requesting permission to depart friendly lines with 18 packs over."

"2-2, 2-2, COC permission granted," squawked the green gear. LT would be rolling out with me and SSgt. would be rolling with Hinde. We would make our way up to the little village next to the compound where the man was killed the evening prior. From there we would move down the hill to the north and ultimately down into the interconnected set of compounds we were warned about. The huts were all flying black flags outside the compounds when we were in the radio tower, so we acted as though the information we were given was solid. As we made our way out of the bazaar and into the open desert, we opened way up in dispersion, in a tactical column. Sgt. Hinde's squad would follow suit until the end of the bazaar and then they would break off to the southeast and skirt my squad's right flank at a few hundred meters.

About an hour or so into the patrol we had just started working up a good sweat when action started crackling over the squad comms; something coming from Hinde's boys regarding suspicious activity. We all started to feel it in the air. The atmospherics of the battlespace started to change drastically. It's hard to explain to someone who has never experienced it. The best analogy I have is, again, bow-hunting big game. There is a different feeling in the air when the thing you're after is among you. The woods settle almost to a complete halt. You no longer pay attention to the sounds of the birds and the sounds of the two squirrels chasing one another back and forth on the forest floor below you. Your ears begin to burn, and the hairs on the back of your neck stiffen. It becomes a sense. The streets once busy become silent, lest the folks left over, in this case wearing long thin garment robes with tight-cut brown and green vests overtop; each of them looking into you with cold eyes filled with hate and opium, wanting to kill you the first chance they get. People ask, *how do you know they wanted to kill you?* It's a look that you will not find just anywhere, but when a person has decided they want to kill you, there is a look that comes with it. Almost a lustful look, an overly confident, blood-thirsty look.

Though there weren't many people meeting us, it was a very creepy feeling that started to arise. At one point my squad made its way up into a large mansion-type building for the area. There were some occupants but zero resistance. The squad managed them well. Most times we would ask them to stay put in the compound until we were moving again. We would put a watch on them and go about our business. If we were in contact, however, things went a bit differently. Sometimes they would stay and sometimes it was safer for them to get the fuck out of Dodge. Once we had the occupants in order, we linked up with Sgt. Hinde and SSgt. Wright over the radio. They were moving up through an open area with spotty micro terrain and canals everywhere. The plan was to travel and overwatch when we established contact with the enemy. LT recommended that we make our way to this little knoll up ahead of our building a bit, not but 25 to 30 meters up. As I started to roll out and move up with the squad, all hell broke loose on Hinde's squad and my squad at what seemed like the same time. We had just broken the crest of the knoll we worked up to, and 1ˢᵗ Squad was caught in the open, moving across a chisel-plowed field; which, if you have never tried to run across a muddy plowed field, is next to impossible to do.

With the crest of the knoll now being peppered, it sent tiny explosions of sand airborne. It seemed like the fire was all over us. Knowing that we couldn't get bogged down, I told the squad to get some dispersion across the crest linearly and on my signal pop and take three to four shots at the small buildings down from the hill. We had to establish fire superiority to relieve the pressure on ourselves as well as Hinde and his boys.

The commands all happen in seconds in a gunfight and we worked to make the best decisions with the information that we had at the time. I ordered the squad to take the hill and I watched my men become lions before my eyes. On command they pushed the hill and started really leaning into the would-be bunker at the base of the hill. Now, actively engaging the enemy, the fight intensified. LT was at the rear of the squad behind me, trying to raise SSgt. on the radio. I remember him trying to get a SITREP from Wright more than once and being told abruptly each time that he was face-down in a chisel-plowed field and would get back to him when able. I remember at some point shortly after we gained fire superiority that LT shouted for me to use a LAW. Cpl. Charette was resistant to giving up his LAW and wanted to take the shot himself, but we were down to one LAW remaining at this point for the squad, and I was the only one who had fired one at the enemy. Also, I wanted to limit the exposure of my men. If someone needed to expose himself for a shot it would be me. The rocket was nearly a direct hit, and again they clapped back at us with a few bursts as they did when we hit the other bunker the week prior. With the fight raging on we called in for support from our mortar section. The mission went up and the mortars came down. They just came down way off-target, enough to constitute calling them off and moving to something a bit surer. When the skids were called in from their holding position, they stacked up and tried to get PID on the enemy in the bunker. When they couldn't see them, it put us in a predicament. I had LCpl. Mackiewicz put a 203-ground marker on the top of the enemy firing position to try to help the birds. He put a money shot on target and the yellow plume rose up in the air. The birds still would not fire.

There are multiple types of controls that are placed on an aircraft and these controls directly correspond with what that bird can do as far as fires, and when it is able to do it. In this situation we didn't have a certified person on the ground to render us "in control" of the bird's ordnance. Thus, the bird had to establish its own Positive ID before releasing its payload. Because the pilots couldn't get PID on the target they had to wave off and try coming in from a different angle. They never established PID and pushed back to the IP. I was pissed they wouldn't fire but I now understand why they didn't. They have their own ROEs and whether I chose to like them or not they had to be followed. I would always mention that to my Marines in times when the boys were getting hasty. Because we aren't animals and because we are good people, we will follow the rules imposed on us. That's what makes us better than them. I say that always to a point, even when I knew some of the rules imposed on us were bullshit. I'd usually piggyback that statement with, "It's better to be judged by 12 than carried by six."

The skids being overhead was enough in and of itself to stifle the enemy to my direct front. As they checked off station, I presumed the fight was going to be coming back again. Bennett got PID on multiple targets on a rooftop way out and off to the north. It seemed to be the origin of the rounds landing all over Sgt. Hinde and 2B's position. Amid the fog the radio started going haywire. It was Sgt. Hinde. He was caught in the open and was shot. As we looked onto their position to our right flank it looked like someone had used a violet smoke grenade in the middle of the field. It was Hinde running around. He had been shot through the drop pouch which detonated his violet smoke grenade that was stored inside, burning through the pouch and burning his leg, making him think he was shot. In the same exchange, one of his team leaders, Cpl. Wiczoric, was shot vertically through his camelback, located on the back of his kit. The only way for that to happen was if he was in the prone position and the round was fired directly over or beside his head. Simultaneously, Bennett and his team opened up on the deep position identified, piling up all three tangos in short manner. When they stopped firing, the battlefield fell silent. With smoke still coming out of the gun barrels, I moved over to the wall I used prior to skirt up to the crest of the hill, peered over toward Hinde's squad and watched the field for several seconds. Over my black gear I contacted Hinde and told him that we sorted the deep threat out and that he was good to move. He copied on the comms and asked, "Are you sure?" *Yes*, I told him, as the field stayed silent except for the noise of the squad behind me changing out for fresh mags and prepping for whatever was to come next.

As Hinde's squad began to move up through the field, echeloning by ones and twos, gunfire again erupted, this time from a different area that was blind to me. As the seconds ticked by, Hinde now actively engaged, and I was going to move down into the village and push the enemy. LT and I weren't about to get pinned down waiting on choppers to get PID. I coordinated with Bennett to set up a support by fire position at the hill and overwatch my movement with the rest of the squad plus attachments into the village. LT would stay back with the SBF and direct traffic, picking up tactical command and control of the SBF team when it was time to move.

Suddenly the radio crackled once more; it was 2Bravo. He was reporting a fallen angel which was our call sign for a friendly KIA, and I was just about to descend the hill with my element. I looked back at LT with emotions in my eyes and yelled, "Who was it? Was it Hinde?" He shook his head and seemed to be disconnected from the moment. Eyes wide open, focused but disconnected. As I turned and ran down the hill into the fight, I could hear Staff Sergeant Wright calling in the nine-line mission to higher. I moved down the hill and back into what I consider a flow state, where my body is functioning at its highest level on all cylinders. My body was in tune with the mission and I was on auto-pilot. I stacked on the door with Charette as the rest of the teams followed suit, including my two EOD techs, who seemed elated to be in another gunfight. As we made entry into each house the SBF position was overwatching our movement from the hill. As we navigated the interconnected village we were clearing and holding our terrain. I got two or three houses in and was running out of men. Everyone was holding except my EOD techs, myself and Charette. We had about a 50-meter opening that we needed to cross to make it into the courtyard of the final building that was yet to be cleared. Once there we could take a moment to breathe, regroup and continue to fight. I assumed the enemy had all broken back a few hundred meters to where the dead enemy lay lifeless on the roof where Bennet left them. But you can't operate in life and death with assumptions.

I was standing in the alley looking north toward the enemy who was firing accurate bursts into the opening that we needed to move through. I slapped Matt on the chest and said, "Last one across loses," and took off running. He passed me within seconds, and I watched as machine gun rounds splashed a ripple in the sand between us. Time seemed to slow down immensely to me, and I thought about my calves and knees that were about to be shredded, still digging as hard as I could; I watched as Charette hit the courtyard wall and button-hooked back out to lay down suppression for me as I entered behind. Upon entry a military-aged male with his werewolf dog came out of the compound fast. I instantly put the dog down with multiple rounds and shifted to the man. With all the excitement and the euphoric emotions of combat I instantly had to take a shit. There were a pair of crates about the size of cinder blocks on the courtyard wall that looked overly inviting. I plopped down to shit on the crates and raised my M4 to hold on the compound inside. Matt was holding security on the opening we came into, as Stannard and Butterfield were moving across now. It was a cowboy kind of a moment as they made their approach, one wielding a service M9 mm firing on the move, knowing damn well he wasn't hitting shit. Like it was scripted, he yelled, "Wyatt fucking Earp." His partner yoked him behind the wall laughing. I finished my shit and continued the clear.

Once cleared, we sorted out the MAM (military aged male) and his dog and consolidated. The consolidation phase of this fight was complicated because of how spread thin the squads were. LT hit me up on the black gear to check in. I replied that we had finished the initial clear but that we were spread thin. He was going to break down the SBF position and consolidate on me the way I understood it. He was overly worried about the last movement we made because in overwatch they lost visibility of us once we crossed the alley. As soon as they lost visibility of us, the gunfire opened up. They were afraid we had been hurt. 2Bravo and Hinde were now making their way to me from the flank clearing to my Marines and then picked them up for me. This situation was also difficult because of how spider-webbed this village was. It was very easy to get turned around in it. I didn't notice it during the gunfight, but the chopper came right over us and picked up the downed man, then tore back out of there. I was trying to orient myself to the map and then to SSgt. Wright who was trying to consolidate on my position. We resorted to "what do you see around you?" I told him I was directly under the building with all the goats on the roof. Everyone got a chuckle, but it was an unmistakable feature.

We were all smoked and needing some good news when I saw Wright moving through the lines with an extra weapon, and someone else with an extra pack. I believe it was Hatch, one of the team leaders in the squad. They all seemed green and almost in shock. It's a humbling experience when you are reminded that you can bleed. To this point, as a platoon, we had lost no one and only had a few casualties but this felt different. LCpl. Hanson from First Squad was wounded badly.

He was initially called in as a fallen angel, but Doc Hernandez managed to bring him back. It was said that though he was faint, he was put on the chopper alive. Nobody talked about what happened and ultimately, we ended the operation and broke back for the firm base to refit. Everyone was clearly shaken up over the day's events and emotions got out a few times on the walk back. Once we returned, I told everyone to break down and clean weapons and got with the team leaders on an after-action report. A little while had gone by and I watch Ssgt. Wright and LT take an unaccompanied walk out of the lines and into the bazaar. I was with Herby on our regular overwatch position that looked back toward the MG bunkers. We smoked and talked about the events of the day; he had been back in the firm base pulling watch on the house with JT's squad. We smoked a while and then got down to the ground and back to our own berthings. I hadn't seen SSgt. Wright or LT come back in from the bazaar before I came down from the roof, but I assumed they must have, as it had been a while. As I walked into Hinde's berthing area to cross through to get to my own, Sgt. Hinde grabbed me by the arm and said, "Hey man I need to talk to you."

"What's up, brother?" I was not expecting the news he was about to share with me.

"I wanted to be the one to tell you that we lost Hanson today. If you need a minute to clear your head you should take that before communicating this to your squad, you know; to keep your composure."

It was good advice for the situation, but I didn't comprehend much after he said Hanson didn't make it. I was immediately flooded with the most powerful rage I had ever experienced. I began to shake and could feel the chemical cocktail drop into my spinal column. This was rage and hate and sadness in a way I had never felt before. With his own lip starting to quiver, he turned and walked away and I fell against the mud wall with my hands. I had now inherited the responsibility that so many before me had to bear, and I didn't want it. I didn't want to tell my men and shatter them; I didn't want to face his family back at home and shatter them; I didn't want to do anything except kill everything.

After several minutes of standing there against the wall I got my hands to stop shaking, and I made my way to my berthing. I had no experience in this and was sure it was going to break me. Most of the guys were in the hut because it was warmer and darker. Some were listening to music with iPods and some were trying to get some Z's. I hadn't cried yet and I was having trouble dealing with the sorrow and anger I was feeling. I felt all the emotions one typically feels when he loses a man on the field, especially when he was helping control movement. I was overwatch for them and told Hinde he was good to move. I felt my chest tighten and blood pressure spike, and I could feel my heartbeat in my eyeballs. I felt like it was my responsibility to inform them completely on all matters and in a timely manner. I never wanted to hide anything from them. As I got closer to the hut I started to fall apart.

I ripped open the tarp door and told everyone to get out, letting the tarp go behind me. Once everyone was out, I screamed as loud as I could, some form of *Fuckkkkk* and then I fell to my knees and began to cry. A headlight flicked on; it was Cpl. Charette. He reached up and grabbed me and asked what was wrong? I fell completely apart, weeping and sobbing for a good 10 minutes before I brought the squad back in. It was unacceptable for me to lose anyone, and now that had become a reality. Everyone knew something was bad wrong and as they all filed in, I told them all about the news. Most of them were good friends with Hanson and shared many memories with him in and out of work. I only knew him briefly, but on my chest-rig still hung his Nalgene bottle as a reminder of his love and thoughtfulness for someone he barely knew just 12 hours before. I often have thought about our last conversation together before departing that morning. We had joked about dying. I never did that again.

The Marines all reacted in much the way I did: there was some crying, there was some rage, there was even talks of a nighttime village patrol...but they were just Marines venting and trying to cope with their loss. When we lose someone in country, that is it. They are gone and gone forever, we don't get the closure that is necessary by way of funeral or wake which is how our mind has always dealt with loss. At best, weeks later after the fight, we will honor the fallen in our own way. It's well after the fight before we get to even begin to heal from these losses. This is necessary as well; you must be able to move past the sorrow to be clear-minded enough to not let it happen again.

More bad news came as Bennet reported Mackie was super sick and could now barely walk. He took his Marine to see Doc Hernandez, and he was evacuated. Down another Marine...

I don't remember much of the rest of the day and evening, but at one point everyone was feeling super down, and those of us not on security post were gathered around a fire in Hinde's berthing area. It was quiet and the sun was fading when one of First Squad's SAW gunners affectionately known as "Bubba" walked out of his hooch and said, "Cheer up fellas!" as he pulled two barn swallows out of his cargo pocket in his FROG pants and threw them up in the air. We all were in awe as the birds flew away and a somber laughter was in the air. It was the ice-breaker we needed to help get past the day's events. In the coming days things would begin to change rapidly.

As the COP was being built and the battlefield was expanding, we were getting spread thinner and thinner. It seemed like every other day there was more space that we needed to occupy. The command was talking about setting up some entry control points (ECP) in order to vet who was traveling in and out of the area, both friendly and enemy, and to be out in the population establishing a presence so all knew we weren't going anywhere. This may give the locals better peace of mind to come home and try to start living again, and to the enemy this simply says, "We're here to bang so let's go!"

In the COC we hashed out how we were going to manage our personnel. The order was to split the squad into two teams reinforced and a team-plus of Afghan Army troops and a corpsman. This would give us the numbers necessary to leave the wire, as well as enough ass to fight and not get annihilated. The ECPs would only be a couple of clicks out from the firm base. A click is 1000 meters, which is uncomfortable, but we had so many air assets and indirect fire assets available to us that though it was uncomfortable, the IDF made us feel better about a shitty situation.

I broke my squad in two, giving the B team to Bennett and keeping Charette's team with me. We would take turns staying at the ECP for five to seven days at a time. Whoever was at the

ECP would maintain the entry point and whoever was not at the ECP would be on the local security patrol missions. I would be the first at the ECP so that I could establish the way things would run, and then I would RIP out with the B team showing them how I wanted it. When I talked to Cpl. Bennett about the move, he was more than comfortable with the shift and we slapped the table on how the evolution would go down. The other squads did much of the same thing. As three squads broke into six teams, we had to maintain two ECPs, security on our main FOB and support a patrolling effort. My knowledge about the movement of the adjacent platoons and units was good at the time, but ever-changing. Being that the GLOC was now open the strip of 608 that runs to our FOB was monitored so it was relatively safe to travel now. Any IEDs that were laced into the road for the push were mitigated by the engineers by now, and since we controlled all traffic on the road, we maintained its safety.

The first trip down to the ECP at 608 was eerie. We still were in active gunfights daily and it was by no means a safe environment outside the wire. But who was I kidding; there was no wire or safe zone. We landed in the middle of the area with helicopters, and now two-plus battalions of Marines and ANA were pushing from the outside of the city in toward us. The enemy had nowhere to run, which meant many times they were amongst us, living-eating-sleeping amongst us. Then there was the constant fear of the local army turning against you. As we pushed out of the bazaar and headed up 608 past the radio tower, it was comforting knowing we now had Marines there constantly, but it was always a constant reminder of what happened on the other side just days ago. I remember walking past the open field leading up to the cemetery and nothing being there except for some HESCO walls set up by the engineers. I wasn't sure how long they would take to build the COP, but I sure was hoping it was soon. Walking down 608 in a staggered column about an hour before sundown, I moved into a minor flow state again, not really coming out of it until we arrived and all the weapon positions were set up and manned, and a post roster had been generated for security. It seemed my body would go in and out of this state of functioning on its own, at all the right times.

We made entry into the compound from which we were to establish the ECP. No one was home, but it was a defendable position with a roof, which in the area was a plus. Not all compounds were built as well as others; some had roofs and some did not. Others had windows and firing ports, some did not. I knew the area was going to be defendable because we had already been there on the morning of the push. The foothold building from day one would now be two doors down from where we were bedded down. There was a total of four posts manning security, essentially one at each corner. For the northwest corner we knocked a hole out of the wall and set up the SAW. The others were a Marine to the north, an ANA to the south and to the east, and either me or Charette always on radio watch and roving to relieve the post standers.

Our job was always to observe the road and record and report all activity of a rare or suspicious nature. We would also sort the enemy out if and when they should attack. These types of position cut down on general enemy activity, IED planting and transporting, and suicide vehicle-borne IEDs (SVBID) from being rammed into our firm bases. The first several days here were slow and miserable. The flies were returning to Marjah and the temperature was edging upward. The vast nothingness and boredom associated with war is not talked about much but is so important to bring in when discussing the real dynamics of it. In the ECP you were essentially confined to a small courtyard and one shed-sized room with wild rabbits living and shitting in it. Your bathroom was an even smaller room where there was a corner you pissed in and a corner you dug a hole and shit in. Later in the deployment we were graced with the emergence of the wag bag. It was a green bag with kitty litter in it used for shitting and proper disposal. So, the conditions alone are horrible, let alone that the average age of the group is 20 or 21, and you're being engaged on a daily basis. Most of the deployments I was on were super slow. This one wasn't that way yet, but we soon would get there.

It was at the ECP when I learned of Charette's vast memory and lyrical love of Biggie Smalls. I walked into the hut late one night after I had been out with the post standers. I enjoyed the nighttime hours, as the stars were so much more plentiful, and it was so quiet it was peaceful. I would go out and bullshit with the guys on post, sometimes for hours whispering back and forth as I would be scanning the landscape through the mini-thermal and night vision devices. Charette always carried a mini-thermal so when I wanted one, we always had it. As I walked into the hut, I hear Matt bust out with, "To all the ladies in the place with style and grace allow me to lace these lyrical douches in your bushes. Who rocks grooves and makes moves with all the mommies, the back of the club sipping Moët is where you'll find me," in his best Biggie voice. I remember him looking up and seeing me and smiling really big. "How long you been there?" We both busted out laughing and reminisced our favorite music and gangster rap into the early morning hours in the middle of the desert.

Each morning we would be ready early as the gunfire would come with the sun. We would watch from the ECP as 1/6 was getting some to the south. We would watch as they would have Warthogs do staffing runs. It's the powerful machine gun wrapped with wings and a pilot dives at the earth and you can physically watch the aircraft getting pushed back as the gun opens up; you see the shots pepper the ground and by the time you hear the shots the pilot is already peeling off on his egress bearing and dropping countermeasures off both sides of the jet – like 10 flares per side simultaneously. I was always fascinated at the thought of the Warthog operating in my theater. I never could have imagined I would not only be fighting a war like this, but never in my wildest dreams would we have this many assets stacked up in direct support of us.

Sometimes the crackling in the morning wasn't 1/6, and the times that it was another company from my battalion, I would intently listen for certain voices of my friends who were unit leaders. Sometimes I could hear my buddy Byron Webb from Lima Company reporting in, and one time he was in gunfight and I recognized his voice calling in a situation report.

The ECP was relatively smooth for our first evolution and the RIP with Cpl. Bennett went well. Each day we would make the patrols and fight the enemy, sometimes in pocket firefights and sometimes in a full-on decisive engagement that could last hours or all day. Keeping the battle space saturated was the idea.

It was amazing to me to watch the COP be built. We would leave for eight to 10 days and by the time we returned there would be so much accomplished. Shortly after we came home, we returned to the new COP. The transition wasn't hard as we didn't have to move very much stuff. We literally were able to carry all our shit on our backs. A few weeks into the split of the squads we had a bit of controversy concerning who was billeted under and over who in the squad hierarchy. It was late at night and handled in squad.

Camp Hanson

Once the COP was fully established there was a conversation about naming it after LCpl. Hanson. Our command wanted us to talk about it and see what the feelings from the guys were. The consensus was overwhelmingly yes. I don't remember what day it was made official, but the COP became known officially as COP/FOB Hanson. Once the battalion moved in it became Camp Hanson. Whenever the battalion came into Hanson our mission was sure to change.

On March 6th I remember using a satellite phone that the EOD techs had been safeguarding and keeping quiet for obvious reasons. I told them I didn't need much time at all but that my wife was having surgery that day and I wanted to check on her. I hadn't spoken to her since a week before the push. They agreed and told me to come get it after my patrol. I retrieved the phone and checked on my wife, and some of the other Marines used it as well that were "in" with the EOD bubbas. I got along great with all our techs. They rolled with us everywhere. The call was short and kind of funny as my wife was still doped up on narcotics from the operation. All in all, she was okay and after some "I love you" talk, we hung up. I didn't like calling home, it risked me being in the wrong mindset, and ultimately it becomes frustrating.

When you have been operating on a squad level for a month or so of straight combat, things that used to be a big deal become small, and things that were small issues disappear completely. When the battalion moves in next door, the small shit becomes big issues, and the big shit becomes catastrophic. I think there is something to be said about the command psyche, regarding how to treat their troops who have been out too long on the front. I often wonder if they knew the gravity of their words and actions when they'd have a squad or platoon on the brink. Maybe it was their way of humbling us all before completely leaving the reservation. It was always like they didn't give two fucks about what you had done last week or today, you were still nothing and nasty. The emotions become stronger the higher up the unit ladder you climb, meaning that outside of your company-proper, going up to the battalion and regimental levels. When they don't know you, they don't care, it seems. When it was announced that we would remain there with the battalion to conduct Civil Affairs Group (CAG) missions and build up Camp Hanson I cringed. I guessed we were chosen because we already were posted here with a built rotation, and we had already been holding the ECPs for a while as well. We knew the area like the back of our hand and had made our presence known over the month, so it makes sense why we would have stayed. With the battalion coming in so did the rest of our gear and the mail, regularly, which we were all stoked about, but outside of that we knew that the propensity for "games" to ensue was rising.

There was word floating around that our platoon would stay right here at Hanson and the rest of our company would be moving out east to a place called Five Points, or COP Reilly. It was stood up by 1st Battalion 3rd Marines just prior to us coming in. "Initial construction was completed in only three days...in honor of Lance Corporal Thomas J. Reilly Jr., the only Marine from 1/3 killed in action during the battalion's deployment to Karmah, Iraq (Tuthill, 2010)." The other platoons in the company had to rip out 1/3 from Reilly and take over the responsibilities of the COP and that was seemingly the direction of the fight. After being on point for the entire invasion we now found ourselves wrapped around the flagpole playing CAG games; things like escorting civilians from place to place to pay money for damages and try to win the hearts and minds of the people. This was the hardest time of the deployment for me personally. I found myself so bored and things became so stupid to me that sometimes I lacked bearing and was downright unprofessional; things like taking shifts on manning the ECP or standing out waving at the locals as they would come and purchase grains and fertilizers from our CAG representatives, always being on guard watching for suicide bombers and/or enemy combatants.

The complacency sets in after several days of this and you must find something to occupy your mind and keep your wits sharp. I often would count every man, woman and child and completely scan them as they approached and retreated, looking for any anomaly from the baseline. Many times, I could enter a "flow state" and maintain complete clarity through the entire day; other times were harder. In the first few weeks the battalion stayed on one side of the camp and we stayed on the other. We would pull all the post watches, man two ECPs, and push out a continuous patrol cycle to saturate the area as a platoon reinforced. Soon after the battalion came in, we were given 3- or 4-gun trucks to set up a mobile section within our own platoon. This would help cover more distance and provide heavier gun support from the road. We were also tasked with visiting and monitoring the farmers and their fields to slow the poppy trade. There were talks about burning fields early on, but that never happened while I was there. The mobile section was set up with Sgt. Hinde's squad with some attached machine gun and assault men. This was mostly due to JT and I having ECP responsibilities with split squads already. This made Herby and his boys mobile.

As the time went by in our new cycle of life, we fought through the boredom and edged on. The battalion sent us two strapping gentlemen to aid us in the daily operations. One was a gunny and one was a captain. I have nothing against officers by any means, but this guy in particular was a complete fucking tool. You know, the kind of officer that has the good-idea fairy posted up as a permanent resident in his tiny little brain. It would have been downright insulting to send us babysitters in my opinion, except that we were really burning it on both ends already and some extra help would have been amazing. It's intensely hard to go from operating every day at 100 miles per hour to coming damn near to a complete halt. We were eager to get back to the fight with the rest of the company but had no clue when or if that would ever happen.

I don't remember a whole lot about Captain America. He was mainly taking the reins with Hinde and the trucks. They would go out and visit a few different FOBs in the AO daily and run batteries, chow and other supplies to our TCP on 605/608 as well as a newly established OP on route Badger that JT and Davis's squad maintained. It was nice not to have to grunt that equipment down to the TCPs anymore, and if we needed batteries or other odds and ends it was only typically a few minutes away. We also were able to self-support an internal quick reaction force (QRF). They would be ready to roll anytime we had squads out, and if they got into a TIC (troops in contact) the trucks would roll out with 240s, a 50-caliber M2 turret mounted, and a heavy Mk 19 that is a belt-fed machine gun that fires 40 mm high explosive dual purpose (HEDP) grenades. This was another one of those weapons that the enemy didn't really understand initially. It would always give me a warm and fuzzy feeling being overwatched by Marine machine gunners. I would always have a smile on my face wanting them to make the mistake of engaging me when the trucks were out and available.

One night the trucks had to make a long movement to resupply the FOB we helped with and drop batteries off at the OP for JT's squad. The OP was much like my TCP in that it had very few defenses and would be manned around the clock. The mobile section had been out a while and the sun fell across the horizon. I was not on the patrol, but this is how the story goes according to the Marines in the trucks...Herby's and LT's accounts...

In a very short time, the camp was so large that we who established it became the silent minority. We did get some mail, our main packs and phone calls occasionally, and briefly the ability to get a hot shower once a week or so if your time and operation schedule permitted. Most of the time they didn't, but we always managed a good water bottle shower on our side of the camp, and then circled up for a bullshit session with the other team and squad leaders or we would bust our Risk or cards and play. Early on as the outcast platoon we had our own privacy. Some of the Marines even made makeshift couches and recliners out of leftover HESCO and different material from constructing the FOB. They made a little NCO lounge in the back of the squad berthing area where we all enjoyed some late-night conversations and would sometimes eat food and chill.

One night while chilling in the lounge I was met by Scotty Davis, Herby, Wolbeck and one or two other team leaders. We stayed up a while bullshitting and telling stories from the past day's firefights and other events. I was biding my time slowly as I had to wake the next rotation of post standers from my squad up to get dressed and ready. As we continued to bullshit and laugh quietly, one of the TLs grabbed a half- to ¾-full bottle of Gatorade off the table and blew ass into it, and without batting an eye handed it to the next person in the circle and continued the story. It was executed with such ease and bliss that the next TL followed in suit and so did the lot of us, five in total, twisting the cap back on quickly each time as to not waste the methane. I didn't even know that the boys had acknowledged what we had done until later.

As the conversation was dwindling down, I checked my watch and jumped up to get my guys moving for post. I woke Grimes up first because he was closer to me and it always took him a bit longer to get moving. I told him to get moving and to grab an MRE, top off his water and then get to post. He yawned big and jumped up, always making some crude fat comment about himself or telling anyone he walked by that they had a healthy-looking dick, whether it was out or not. I went to the other hooch and repeated instructions to Minime who was already up and moving. By the time I made it back to the lounge area, Grime was just then kitted up. I told him time was up and to get to post. He said okay and asked if we had anymore Gatorade. Without missing a beat one of the TLs grabbed the methaneade and tossed it over to him after a shake saying, "This is the last one, but since you're going on post you can have the rest." Everyone was straight up locked into some kind of bearing that we didn't know we possessed, waiting as to not ruin the prank. We didn't intend for it to be Grimes, but we were going to get our seven laughs. He was super thankful. We all thought he was going to take it to post with him and then later the fruits of our labor would be laughed about a little at best. Instead, Mike hurriedly spun the cap off and without thought or hesitation upended the bottle and drank the entire thing in a few seconds. After he brought the bottle down and swallowed the last gulp, he summoned up a large belch and then looked at all of us falling the fuck out at this point, defeated. He had a sort of confused look on his face, lapping his tongue, and said, "That Gatorade tastes like ass!" We didn't have to go far into the weeds with why it may have tasted that way, as we were all rolling, clutching our stomachs and gasping for air. He turned around and said nothing, walking into the black night towards his post. Grimes was a great Marine but acquired the unofficial duty of being the whole platoon's comedic relief. He was always a good sport with things like that, even though that one was just him by dumb luck.

Late at night when all the patrols would come back inside the wire, we would break out the cards and play Texas hold 'em. Everyone who played wanted to bet money, but you aren't supposed to. The only way to do it is to keep books and hope you get paid back at home. It was far more instantly gratifying to come up with nasty concoctions of left-over consumables and have them drink or eat it for payment once knocked out of the game. One time I lost early in the game and the payment was to drink a half a Dixie cup worth of soy sauce. I threw up several times that night, and still to this day must take soy sauce in small doses. Who the fuck has soy sauce mailed to them in country, I wondered?

Herby had to pull a prank on a higher-up one night as payment for getting knocked out of the game. The higher-up that he was to prank was a gunnery sergeant that was attached to us from the battalion to aid in the daily operations. I personally think he was sent to keep an eye on us too. He was a cranky old bastard, always pissing and moaning about something. He was noticeably disgruntled toward the end of his career and didn't give much of a fuck what others thought about his views. He never really gave us any grief, but he was mostly negative from what I remember. Herby was tasked by another member of the game to deliberately wake the gunny up by completely unzipping his hooch and screaming. I think his response to the challenge was, "Don't threaten me with a good time, motherfuckers." He left to accomplish his black op, and we followed to watch the execution phase from afar. It was sometime around 2 a.m. and the old man had been buttoned up in there for some time. Herby started off by going to his own hooch which was a squad tent, cots on both sides and an aisle down the middle, and he poured some water in a small package of Apple Jacks he received in the mail and sat it on the side of his iso mat and sleeping system. He then opened his sleeping system and started to undress. I didn't see the genius in his plan for a few minutes, but he stripped down to his green PT shorts and stood up. He had set up a disguise and it was perfect. Next, he crept up to the target tent and set the plan into action. I laughed so hard that my cheeks were sore. He grabbed the zippers and all at once flung the door open screaming and shaking the tent briefly, then he hauled ass to his hooch and dove into his bag. With only a little time left, he hurried the cereal bowl (soggy by now) onto his chest and closed his eyes. As the old man tore out of his one-man hooch spitting and cursing, I couldn't help but watch and laugh from the COC... The old man slugged through each berthing, cursing and threatening everyone, but no one was awake, or so it appeared. It was never really mentioned after that day, but it was never again a task to complete. That was a one-time only punishment. This would only be the start of the games that were played. Most of the deployments I was on, the machine gunners would always have a game or a "tradition" they kept up where they would give out a 7.62 projectile (the actual bullet) to everyone in the MG section before leaving home. They would use pliers at the range and pull off the projectiles. The game is that you must come back with the round. If you don't you have to fulfill some punishment such as covering a bar tab or being the DD the first night back.

It was never something cruel, just fun. As the years went on it became harder and harder for the gunners to get the rounds back through Customs to the US. Many times, I saw the gunners wear their round on a piece of 550 cord around their necks. When Customs got too bad, they resorted to different measures, such as mailing them home. I suppose every unit has their little traditions and games; some are more extreme than others. In my experience in the Marines and especially Kilo 3/6, I never took part in or witnessed an extreme case. I didn't believe in hazing Marines, and I never got off on demeaning someone else, but shenanigans and games I was always good with. I remember one time after we came home from Marjah, I was an instructor at the School of Infantry and I was on my way into work, coming down the stretch to Camp Gieger, when two boots ran out close to the road and knelt beside it. I was jamming my tunes, watching, and thought nothing of it. About 100 meters away now in my truck one of the Marines runs across the street and begins tying something to a stake and then runs off. Simultaneously the other Marine does the same and runs off. I guess it was that I hadn't been home long enough or something because I locked up the brakes just long enough to see them laughing their asses off. I got "gotted" for sure. They in fact were just simulating tying a wire across the street, there was in fact no danger to my truck or to me. I was fuming at the time mainly because of embarrassment, took a direct right turn into the advanced machine gunner parking lot, jumped out of the truck and said, "Get over here Marines!" They were still smirking as they ran over to me and went to parade rest. I commenced to tell them that it was the best prank I had seen in a while. We all laughed, and they went about their way.

In Marjah the pranks and games got a bit more incongruous due to the setting and available time and energy. If you were going to use your last remaining energy for the day on a prank, you make damn sure it's a good one. You must be able to get your seven laughs and then some if you're going to set up a prank or scheme in country. One of the pranks that took place in country was the "Don" of all pranks witnessed throughout my entire career. It started on Camp Hanson, so it seems fitting to talk about. I will start by saying that I never to this day have found out who did this, and I'm pretty sure nobody else ever did. One night I got a funny story told to me in the smoke pit from the "Lance Corporal underground" that I was sure couldn't be true. The word was that someone on the main side of the camp was popping wag bags. A wag bag is a small green bag that comes with a sort of kitty litter in the bottom. The bag comes rolled up tight and easy to stow. These bags are taken out of any camp or patrol base where the Marines won't have a head to utilize. If you're on the camp they are stowed in the makeshift heads built out of plywood and 2x4s. The way the head is constructed is there is a 2x3-foot section at the bottom, cut out where the wag bag hangs visibly from the back side of the unit. The reason this hole is cut there is to slide half of a 55-gallon barrel under it to piss and shit in when you don't have wag bags. When the barrel fills up you send the Marines to burn and stir it with JP8 diesel fuel. Being that we had bags at this point, in the engineer's opinion, there was no need to close said holes. So, popping a wag bag is where someone is shitting with the wag bag hanging, and someone else sneaks close and slaps the bag from the bottom, sending shit, piss and kitty litter up into the backside and unfortunately sometimes through the opening of the person shitting. This probably wouldn't have been very funny or even enough to gain traction across the battalion, except that it was happening to the battalion sergeant major. It was rumored that he was sending nastygrams out on all nets looking for the "bag-popper" as this prank didn't just happen one time. As a matter of fact, it was rumored to have happened several times. For a prank on a senior staff member, in country, on a deployment like this, of this magnitude, it's no wonder, Sir, why you have kept your secret safe for so long. My hat is off to you and the energy you utilized for such a fait accompli.

I can't imagine trying to sit down after a long day of work to take a shit before bed and getting halfway through when a loud and violent pop shakes my porta-potty house; at the same time my own urine and shit fly up at me as if they wanted to dive back in to where they came from. It's not like you're going to bust the door open fast in this situation to catch the perpetrator. Oh, and God forbid this was what we call an "alone-time" shit or a motivated shit. Can you imagine? It's again the small wins for the grunt at the tip of the spear that gets us through. I remember laughing until I cried in the smoke pit that night, and then every time thereafter when word would come that it happened again. I could just envision it happening and I would double over laughing. Later in my life I still laugh, but I wonder more now who it *must have* been. Someone with intimate access to the command and their schedule. Someone who must have worked for or with the SgtMaj. closely and knew his shitting schedule. I assume it may have been either someone he wronged in one way or another or someone in his circle that didn't fear being caught or punished. This leaves the officer corps and a select number of senior enlisted...and the JUMP section of Marines that escorted the command every day. Either way, such an epic tale.

It became a thing in most of the squads where we wanted any mission leaving the camp, whether it was a security patrol or a resupply run to the bazaar, or even sometimes when I volunteered to take the new Lioness outfit of female Marines to introduce them to the AO. They were stone-cold female Marines. I never remember their names as we didn't operate but a few times together, however, I think some of the guys may have gotten to know them. We all lived on the same base and they would frequently be helping down at the CMOC (Civilian-Military Operations Center) near the gate. They would do all the pat-downs and conversation-having with the female locals. If we needed to apprehend a female, they would do all of that. It's amazing the lengths that we as a country go to, even at war, to ensure that respect is given to the enemy and local populations. I agree with this principle and hope that Marines in general continue to as well. In my mind it is the only thing that separates us from the animals. In the Pacific campaign, US Marines were dismembered, some left with their own penises cut off and stuffed in their mouths and other places. That is animalistic and downright evil. In that place, we chose to respect our enemy.

Between the constant patrol cycle, the CMOC detail and trips down to the ECP, there wasn't much down time. What time we did have typically got fucked with because complacent Marines make stupid choices. It was around this same time that I started to PT with LT. Every day before I would go to the gate we would work out for an hour or so. We would run, then come back and conduct some sort of CrossFit workout. One day the workout we decided on was kettlebell swings. I was not in great shape before leaving to come here but was better now and able to hang with LT for a bit. We did our workout and I was smoked. I thought we were finished but LT said no way.

We both started at the same time with the same weight kettlebell on what we called a kettlebell challenge. The first one to stop swinging properly was the loser. I don't know exactly how long we went for, but at some point, we both knew the other was not going to stop, so we mutually agreed to end the challenge. I was so sore for the next several days. Another time LT had a wild hair up his ass and wanted to fight everyone. This is a big deal in the grunt community. We ground fight and grapple all the time. I guess it's an alpha's way to keep your shit quick, maybe also to challenge yourself, get a workout or establish dominance. I fought LT for a while and I was so afraid he was going to kill me that I tried to kill him back. We rolled and rolled, choked each other and broke out and then rolled some more. LT ended up tapping me out with a rear naked choke after he took my back in an exchange. It was a good fight, though, and respect between us grew.

For a few weeks we muddled through the menial CAG operations until one day I was called up to the COC to get a patrol brief from the LT. I showed up with my map gear and my comms. I was informed that I would be escorting the two CAG civilians to a few compounds in Shinnywal, and a compound or two on the outskirts. I got my coordinates and referenced my GRG map, thinking it should be an easy trip. I went back to my berthing hooch and gave the locations to my point man and Cpl. Charette. "Get acquainted, boys," I said as I handed them the GRG. I pulled up a cot and let Wetzel know how I wanted the route to come into Shinnywal, and roughly where I wanted to set up our stops. You have to say "roughly" because when it falls apart, you are so locked in on the one plan that you may hinder the unit's ability to improvise on the move. I looked at Charette and told him we would be taking the CAG civilians out, one man and one woman. He gave me a shit-eating grin and said, "She hot?" We laughed and I told him I didn't know. During PCCs and PCIs, I told the boys we would be running an escort mission and that there would be multiple stops within Shinnywal. I told them to keep their eyes peeled and head on a swivel. Just before I concluded the pre-combat checks and inspections our two 25-year-old CAG officials showed up. The female was fit and not bad on the eyes for most of the guys. Her partner was fit as well, and neither one had weapons. As they strolled up to the COC they smiled and held out their hands to shake. We shook and prepared to step. I told the civilians that I would accommodate them the best I could, but that ultimately this was my show and I expected them to abide by that.

Right out of the gate we have a couple hundred meters of open ground before running into the village. All was going smoothly until we came into Shinnywal and the male CAG official tried to get one of my guys to stop clearing courtyards and alleys with his weapon. This was not good advice, and these were my men, not his to command. My Marine grabbed him by the arm and had fire in his eyes when he told the dude what would happen if he touched the Marine's rifle again. I intervened and had a "come to Jesus" meeting right there on the spot with both CAG reps. I told them that whatever they thought about this place and these people was their own prerogative, but how these missions would be conducted by my squad would be entirely my decision. Furthermore, my Marines would remain in the first block of war until I saw fit.

One day out on the gate, my squad had just gotten done running a security patrol down to the land bridge bazaar for creature comforts and to establish a presence in the area and gauge atmospherics amongst the locals. Gauging your atmospherics simply is patrolling your sector and observing the local populace. After several days you can begin to build the general baseline for the atmospherics of your AO (Area of Operation). The baseline is the normal, everyday behavior that the population maintains on an average day or night. The longer you are in an area the more detailed you can form your baseline. The better your baseline is in your AO, the easier it becomes to notice anomalies in your baseline. A simple example would be on a regular day when your atmospherics are good, the locals are moving about and kids are playing in the bazaars. An anomaly would be taking a patrol into the bazaar and suddenly there are no longer kids playing and the only people you see are MAMs moving sneakily in and out of the buildings. This is called a shift in the atmospherics. The anomaly is typically followed by the sound of explosions and gunfire. It does something to one's nerves and ultimately one's mind when people you see and greet every day will smile at you today and try to blow you away tomorrow. Profiling and gauging atmospherics became a daily habit that became second nature and I'm sure saved lives.

Following the patrol, we had to pull post out at the ECP to Camp Hanson. JT's squad would be coming down to relieve us in a bit and I was trying to hold my piss until then. I had to piss before we stepped out on patrol and just didn't, which I knew better than to do. I had been looking at the minutes tick by on my watch as I watched the snaking line of locals leading up to our personnel search area, where the boys were patting everyone down and escorting them through the process to enter the compound in search of work, food or cash. They had a very restricted area that they could travel in. Never into the camp proper. They would be run through an identification system to register them in our databases. This also flags them as a terrorist if we had profiled them before in one of our detention camps in Iraq or Afghanistan.

Just as the time was closing in on our relief changeover, I heard a muffled gunshot from the back side of the camp. Following the shot, I heard the black gear go off. Scotty Davis was trying to raise 2B on the internal comms. My heart dropped as there wasn't much else being said. "Good thinking," I thought. Don't blast a fuck-up over the battalion net unless 100 percent necessary. I knew that something bad had happened, probably a negligent discharge or something. Hoping that it wasn't something too bad, I went back to monitoring the folks in line. I had to piss so badly at this point that I was seriously contemplating pissing my pants. I weighed it out, pros versus cons. It was not horrible weather out so it wouldn't warm me up or cool me down at all, but it would be so relieving. I would smell like piss for sure, and if this gunshot becomes something serious, I wouldn't be relieved on time if at all, and that meant I would go all day covered in my own piss. As my mind wandered down that rabbit hole the black gear squawked again. This time it was 2B calling for me to come up to meet him.

At the top of the CAG area away from the ECP I met up with SSgt., where he informed me that while JT's squad was prepping to relieve my guys, one of his SAW gunners accidently sent his bolt home with a round on the feed tray, sending the one round into action and out of the barrel at 3,000 feet per second. The bullet must have ricocheted off something just before entering his squad leader's leg. JT would be getting evacuated by chopper shortly to go back to Leatherneck to get patched up. He only took a fragment or two into his calf. It reportedly didn't even take him off his feet, and as he was walking away to get medical attention, he told his gunner he was going to beat his ass if it happened again. I laughed an unassuming laugh and shook my head. My urge to piss was hitting an all-time peak as I walked back down to the gate. All the way down to my post I again contemplated pissing my pants, again weighing out the pros and cons. Eventually I decided it was okay just to hold it if I could and if not relieved, I would go ahead and soil my trousers.

I thought back to one evening when my section of the squad was down at the TCP established at the intersection of 605 and 608, at the foothold building from the invasion. It was one of the first cycles we had done at the TCP. I was awoken by Cpl. Charette with wide eyes, firmly pressing on my leg. "We got trouble," he said. I got up, quickly and quietly pulling on my kit, pulling my Oakley desert boots on and leaving my pants behind. I whispered to him to fill me in. He told me that the post standers, both Marines and ANA, were tripping out because they were hearing movement. It was the wee hours of the morning when there shouldn't be very much movement at all. It was a very quiet place at night. The problem with the area of the TCP is that there were roads and canals on all sides of us and a building on the north side of our compound that was only about five feet away from our outer courtyard wall. At the time there was still a farmer and his family dwelling in it. The Marines on post were wielding an M249 SAW, and the rest small arms and grenades, a typical loadout. The ANA had a similar loadout; they just had many RPGs to add to it. Point is, I felt more than comfortable to exit the wire to investigate.

My legs were cooled by the 3 a.m. breeze as Charette and I moved out of the north exit to clear out the suspected area. He was running point with his M4/M203 and I had the number two position with my M4. We made a direct and methodical movement out the rear of the compound and around to the east wall facing the roads. Next, we moved across the street to check the canals and culverts. It was one of the creepiest situations I had experienced. Both Charette and I could tell someone was amongst us but we found nothing to prove it. They were very skilled at getting in and out of an area but were they this good, I wondered? The night was a sleepless one for the both of us as we waited up, eyes peeled, until the sun came up begging him to make a mistake. We could feel morning approaching as the temp began to climb and the other Marines began to move around. The neighbor that was living out of our side gate informed some of the Marines that he had be given a letter by a "night rider" and he was afraid for his kids' lives. I thought very little about it.

Trying to hold my liquid I scanned Route Cathey to the south, directly mirroring our ECP. It was common to have bud guys moving about down there, and occasionally, if you were sharp, you would catch something. One day early on, when the CAG ops were in their infancy, we witnessed a man on Route Cathey "digging in" an IED, presumably. As we watched with anxious eyes trying to get PID on the weapon so that we could engage, he exploded. He was the first person I had ever seen explode. I remember not thinking it bothered me at the time because he was trying to kill us. Later that night I scribbled in my notebook a short poem outlining the events I watched unfold. I called it "The Marjah Paradox." It reads:

The Marjah Paradox

The Taliban break in at night and capture a farmer and his entire family,

They tell the farmer to go plant a bomb outside the Marine base, or they will rape and kill his family.

The farmer attempts to plant the bomb as any father would, and admirably so.

The 19-22-year-old Marine will kill the farmer every time, and admirably so.

The older I've gotten the more I believe the words I felt at that time. Some of these people were good people stuck in an impossible situation. They are doing their best to survive in a world that is one hundred times more violent and ruthless than us privileged Americans are accustomed to. What, I ask, would you do if you were put in the farmer's shoes? My gripe is not with killing the farmer. I have been that guy. It's with the evil man that manipulated someone with their children and threats of violence. The person that does this is pure evil, in my opinion.

Since the rest of the platoons in our company pushed out to Five Points, we had been grinding and trying not to get into too much trouble. "Trying" is the key word in that sentence. There was word that we would be seeing some of our brothers from the company at Hanson today; we were told they set up an official memorial service to honor all our fallen warriors thus far. Hanson and Currier being amongst the fallen, we would all be in attendance; both of whom I was on the battlefield with when they were killed. This would be a first for me, and like many other firsts, I wasn't sure how I would react. I knew that I owed it to myself and to the fallen to react in whichever manner felt natural.

We all gathered in a small area carved out for the ceremony, and the group was called to order. Everyone snapped to attention in an instant. First sergeant began to address the group. The hardest part of the ceremony for me has always been "roll call." This is where first sergeant begins to call out roll, naming a few Marines in the group, who would firmly respond "present." About two or three names in the name of a Marine killed in action are read something like this, "Lance Corporal Hanson (long pause), Lance Corporal Hanson (long pause), Lance Corporal Matthias Numand Hanson..." each time louder and on the final time with a quivering lip. With no response he is honored and recorded.

As each Marine was read off, I wept. I left my Oakleys down and cried hard. I remember feeling the hot sun on the back of my neck, and the stiff breeze making the sweat and tears on my face feel cool. My glasses were fogged up by the time the last name was recorded. I sniffed and wiped my nose. The next part of the ceremony was approaching the cross-shaped memorial, constructed with a Kevlar on top of the buttstock of a rifle bayonetted into a sand bag. At the bottom of the cross-shaped memorial was a pair of combat boots, positioned open, at a 45-degree angle just as the yellow footprints those Marines stood on when getting off the bus at boot camp. The dog tags of each of the fallen were then center-marched and hung from the pistol grip of the rifle. Lance Corporal Travis Vuocolo was the Marine who hung Hanson's tags. We all then formed a line and approached the memorials, each man taking time to say good goodbye in his own way.

I walked up and for each Marine I knelt and said a silent prayer. When I got to Hanson, I knelt and grabbed his tags, brought them to my forehead and said a prayer. I closed my prayer by thanking him for his courage and sacrifice to something greater than himself, and then I apologized for not being better. I stood and continued to the end where I was a mess. I was in a sort of daze behind the shades when I saw the CO. Captain Biggers approached me and grabbed my shoulder. He asked if I was okay, and told me when I was ready he needed his anvil back. He said that Sgt. Harms was his hammer and I was his anvil, or something like that. I took that as a compliment and wiped my tears. "I am ready right now Sir!" He smiled and said he was going to get something arranged and we parted ways. It was either a great tactic to get my head out of the ceremony or a true compliment. Either way, I took it as affirmation that I was faring well as a squad leader amongst the command element. It reinvigorated me to get back to the fight and to stay sharp.

The ceremony had brought back the rage and anger I felt on the days we lost Hanson and Currier. The thought of getting the hell away from the flagpole and back to the fight was pleasing to think about. Now at 32 years old it's odd that I still feel the same.

Why would one rather be out of the wire and operating in dangerous territory daily, living and eating like shit, being on the brink of death, versus being close to the battalion where it is safer and has all the available amenities? For me, the amenities meant nothing when I knew that my company brethren were out of the wire fighting daily. It made me think about a quote from the book "On Combat" by LtCol Dave Grossman. The book had been on the Commandant's reading list for corporals and sergeants when I was coming up. There is an excerpt that does a great job of explaining the emotions in such a situation.

"You stay despite your tears because the team, your new family of brothers and sisters, truly needs you, and you'd rather die than let them down. You live in the moment, slowly realize your own mortality and also your steadily rising desire to cling to and fight hard for every second of it. You keep your focus, your "game face" on, and you don't allow yourself the luxury of "too much reflection" or a moment's "daydreaming" about home, loved ones, the future of your return. You privately fear that such a moment of inattention may be your last, or worse, because of you, a comrade's last (Grossman)."

For me, it was simple: I didn't want to attend anymore ceremonies like this one and lose any more of my friends. It was clear that this was impossible, running CAG ops three to four clicks from the company fight. I couldn't help from here and it burned. If all was on the up-and-up, though, the CO would be making moves to get us out of there. I have often told friends and family that for me, war was easy compared to being at home. You didn't have to worry about drama, what friends are real and which ones aren't, who would give their last breath for your safety and who wouldn't. If you needed help you got it instantly. There was a hierarchy, but it was built for us in Kilo almost with a tribe mentality. Over there, nothing matters but locating, closing with and destroying the enemy. The run-of-the-mill daily drama and daily stress that one experiences at home just doesn't exist. I was finding that the closer I was to the flagpole, the more of that stress I was experiencing.

There was a short period of time following the ceremony where we talked with one another and then all at once the time was up and it was back to reality. The other platoons and the company command were all headed back to Five Points and we were headed back to the outcast section of Hanson. That what we called *ourselves* amongst ourselves. We felt like we were the outcasts of our company left to rot and die at the flagpole as the rest of the company drove the enemy back and continued fighting a war. At least the captain had given us some comforting words about getting back to the fight, and we would hang on those words until they came true.

The longer we were at Hanson, the more eager we were to leave. Every day consisted of the camp becoming more and more vast as new equipment came rolling through the gates daily. We were still experiencing pockets of resistance in the AO with the occasional firefight, though, especially if you went looking for it.

Five Points

I don't remember the date, but it wasn't long after the ceremony when I was notified by LT and 2Bravo that we would all be heading out to meet up with the company at Five Points. I would be going first with my squad in trucks and then the rest of the squads would RIP in the new guys for the camp and meet me in a couple of days out at the new COP. I was super stoked to get back out to the action and I hurried back to the squad berthing to inform the boys about the news. I don't guess they were ever as excited as I was to get back to the action. I wasn't a ribbon-chaser, by any means, but I lived for the job and to lead Marines in combat ushering out American resolve 5.56 millimeters at a time. Many of the guys in my charge weren't driven that way. Some might have liked the amenities and security provided by the battalion, which means the news may not be what they really wanted to hear. Regardless of how everyone felt about the move, it was absolutely happening. The next morning, we would be catching a ride out to our new home for possibly the duration of the pump.

Making a big movement, or a permanent move in country or out, is a big deal. You must check, re-check and the check again to ensure you aren't leaving anything or anyone behind. I learned briefly the hard way years earlier in Iraq what it feels like to lose a Marine. I was new to the squad leader game but still handling my business. It was a particularly dark night and we were conducting a patrol to one of the Iraqi Civil Order Police stations to resupply them, gauge atmospherics at night and show our presence in the area.

In my patrol brief I covered the exact route through the spider-webbed alleys that wound through the town of Karbala. It still had the look of death and rubble from the "Steel Fist" tour before I had arrived. I also covered the weather and the fact that we would have close to no ambient light to work with, so we would be closing our dispersion a bit. When we broke for PCCs and PCIs everyone seemed ready, awake, alert. The patrol was a cold one. Just outside the ECP I slipped on an iced-over puddle and busted my ass. Now pissed off and wet, I climbed to my feet and smirked, thinking how the fuck am I falling on ice in Iraq...? The patrol was smooth and the chai we drank at the IP station was warm and sweet, as the IPs would put enough sugar in the small cup to completely fill the bottom half an inch as if to have a snack at the end. It was always so good.

We were on our way back to the COP going through a particularly rough area of the town, where the alleyways closed to about a double arm's-length width. Sometimes the walls were taller than us and other walls you could look over to the other side. It was much like Shinnywal in Marjah. As we snaked out of the housing alleys and made the road, I turned around to count my guys out of the village and up to the road. It was a very confusing route and I always stopped here when taking this route to count. When I came up a Marine short, I instantly panicked. It was Lance Corporal Lane, a small, timid kid who I hoped now more than ever had paid attention to the route and lost Marine plan in the patrol brief.

My lost Marine plan for that deployment was to seek cover in the vicinity of where you realize you are turned around, and if it is dark out, turn your IR laser on the PEQ15 and point it straight above yourself. Thank God Lane paid attention. I scanned back to the village above the houses with my PVS7s and saw the IR beam. I turned the squad around and went back to retrieve my Marine. Everything worked out okay that time, but it was a lesson in being more careful. Not to mention Marjah 2010 was not Karbala 2007.

Conducting my checks in Marjah was a bit more complicated, as we had much more gear on this one, and we were typically staying outside the wire or only coming inside it briefly. All batteries, radios, gear, clothes, food, rounds, water...all carried on your person. Touching everything for sight counts was next to impossible most of the time because you were rarely in a position where you had everyone or everything that was serialized with you. When I think back on it now, I can't believe we didn't lose more shit than we did.

We would be catching a ride to Five Points with the Company JUMP section and I would meet up with Sgt. Harms and

Sgt. Young to get spun up and introduced to the AO. Sgt. Harms was a ginger like me, and he was a hell of a warfighter. He was a squad leader in an adjacent platoon. Sgt. Young was a machine gunner by trade, but as a section leader, was pushing his squad in Marjah as a line squad conducting daily patrols. Both men I owe a debt of gratitude to, as they helped me more in and out of the Corps for inspiration and tactics than they could possibly have known.

The ride out to Five Points in the MRAPs was nice. My squad had been on foot since we stepped off the bird a couple months earlier. It's funny to think about it now, but I wrote in my journal when arriving at Five Points that the ride felt like we were going warp speed. I think the top speed we hit was 35 to 40 mph, but it felt unbelievably fast. When your top speed for 60 days or so is three to four mph on the God-given Cadillacs, 35 to 40 mph takes some getting used to again. But we would not be back on trucks as far as I knew. This was just a lift to the next arena, essentially.

As Five Points first came into view, it was fitting that they named it Five Points. It reminded me of my home in Ohio. Just down from my house is an intersection where five roads all come together. At home it was affectionately known as Five Points as well. By having a forward operating position here, the Marines could monitor five roads at once; however, the risk of having SVBIDs was inherently higher by being so close to so many roads. We hadn't seen any SVBIDs yet, but you never know. They were more than capable of making such bombs. We had already encountered directional wall charges, daisy-chained jug IEDs made of ANAL (ammonium nitrate and aluminum), and dual initiating devices for command detonation. Why would we ever discount the ability to try it all in a vehicle?

As we rolled through the serpentine entryway, the moondust billowed up like smoke from a housefire. The sand was so fine that it created this moon-dust type of cloud out of the fine powders sand. When the weather started to warm up, there was no longer the nightly condensation holding down the finely powdered sand. Just the thought of huffing that shit for the next several months or even possibly for the rest of my life made me laugh an uneasy laugh.

We continued to wind around the ECP (Entry Control Point) until the FOB opened and we came to a stop. I jumped down out of the truck and told the team leaders to organize the boys and gear; I was going to check in at the COC and find out what the marching orders were. They all gave me a nod and off they went. Being by myself was not unnerving as I was so anxious to get back to the fight. I would be missing my platoon but only for a brief time. They were still ripping in the new units at Hanson. As I walked up to check in, I noticed that the COC had been set up nicely. It was a good-sized command tent with big-ass antennas all around it, and a company gunny compound to the right flank, full up with barriers and C-wire. Gunny housed all the Gatorade and hot rations in his little compound, I suppose in order to ration it. Most of the Marines at Five Points were either on post, asleep from being on post or patrol, or on patrol. There were two well-built mortar pits in the center of the COP and a large telescopic camera called a GBOSS. It was able to see 360 degrees, zoom in and zoom out, go white hot or black hot for thermal night vision, and it was also equipped with a laser that would give you the exact grid location of where you shot it. This machine is an amazing help on the battlefield when used correctly. If one was inclined to help a unit on the field, they could have 10-digit grid locations for fire missions or support birds instantly. The device is also optimal when you have units out of the wire to watch their backs and ensure the enemy isn't trying to plot on them. I had seen devices like this one in previous deployments, but they were always used for something other than what they were supposed to be used for.

I brushed back the tent flap doors that were holding in all the AC for the command tent. When I walked in, I instantly got cold. I had worked up a sweat in the short walk up here. It must have been 100 degrees already, worse in the direct sun. Walking into the COC was like walking into a deep freezer. I was so cold that my sweat streams on my face got ice cold and then disappeared quickly. A chill ran up my entire body. The first person I saw was the CO and we shook hands and talked about the upcoming planned events in the AO and chatted about certain areas of interest he wanted us to visit on our brief walkabout. He called in Sgt. Young and told him to take me out and introduce me to the AO. I would be traveling with his squad for the first patrol and then I would take my squad after. This patrol was intended to cover the northeast sector of the AO and familiarize me with the area.

Sgt. Young pointed up at the map on the wall and showed me how things worked with it. It was more than a map. The command center was still a work in progress, but they had a very nice fire mission and checkpoint board put up on the wall. (A fire mission is a mortar mission called in by friendly troops. The mortars are dropped and the locations of where they were dropped are recorded. In case a mission happens to be needed again, the gunline already has the data required to have rounds on target immediately.) It made the life of the unit leader easier when trying to arrange his pre-planned fire missions, as well as his checkpoint and patrol routes. It was a giant GRG (Grid Reference Guide) of our entire Company AO. Then the staff plotted all the fire missions used thus far. Then they added a bunch of pre-planned fire missions in trouble areas on the map. It was pure genius, whoever made it happen. I watched and studied the map, marking down on-call fire mission reference numbers in case we needed some help. What was good about the on-call targets was that they were virtually on every bridge, on the main intersections and on the prominent houses identified as houses where Marines had taken fire from.

The COP itself was not impressive but it was in a good location. It was built just like Camp Hanson with the HESCO walls, double-stacked, and machine gun posts in every flank and corner position. Inside the walls was a burn pit, a section of makeshift shitters made of wood and a shower house with a pallet floor. This is where you could go to have some privacy for your water bottle showers. There was a berthing section for all the platoons, and then a GP tent dedicated to the new ANA Kandak who just arrived shortly before my squad.

At the COC, large OE antennas reached high into the sky, sending out signals of life and death on an almost constant basis. The GP tent on the inside was straight sophistication, with targeting boards and a comms section dedicated to tracking patrols and communicating with higher-ups. Beside the comms table was a 60-inch flat-screen TV hooked up to our GBOSS. The GBOSS was a telescopic camera with night vision and infrared and laser capabilities. They were supposed to be used to watch out for friendly patrols while outside the wire but were typically used to spy on Marines for not wearing the proper PPE or in case they wanted to berate a squad because of the way a real-life break contact maneuver looked... Then there was also a prison gym set up with a few dip bars and then a bunch of heavy chains, no doubt stolen from somewhere. Our CO was a CrossFit nut, so he was surely going to get us more equipment if he could. The gym was spitting distance from the GBOSS, and flanking the gym was Gunny's compound. This was the place where Gatorade went to die and lose its color. There were a few rows of concertina wire set up to enhance the protection of the gunny himself and the supplies he would maintain during our stay. There was shade cast over both the gym and the entire gunny compound by some camo netting. I tried to not spend much time in this area as I didn't get along with Gunny Mack very well. Not that we hated each other, we just started off on a bad foot is all. In the middle of the FOB was the 81 mm mortar pits where our tubes were already sunk in and prepared to rain steel when needed. The position was textbook and served as a secondary smoke pit when necessary. Sometimes you would see the NCOs gather at the mortar pit and the juniors at the designated smoke pit.

All in all, the outpost was going to do just fine. It's all we had. Over the next several months this would become our safety net and home to bounce in and out of. After a day or so of getting to know the post, we took out our first patrol. It was my squad and Sgt. Young's squad. Sgt. Young was senior to me and had a good head on his shoulders. He was a machine gunner by trade but was operating his boys as a regular infantry squad here in Marjah.

On the first patrol out, we were visiting a few key locations that he wanted to point out to me and the boys, mainly wadi-crossing areas that were safe to use and some to stay away from. He also showed us the key mosques and some other key terrain features such as areas where previous gunfights erupted. Following the elongated patrol, we came back to the base and started to debrief with each other.

At some point I met up with Sgt. Harms and shared a heated-up honey bun and discussed tactics. He said he was thinking about different ways to catch up to the enemy. The enemy was much more mobile than we were, and they had mopeds and vehicles to bound out of range with quickly. We tossed a few ideas around and staggered out to the smoke pit. I pulled out a Newport and lit it, plopping down in the sand and leaning back on the sandbags resting my M4 on my chest. I took a long drag and looked at Joey Harms. "What the fuck should we do about this little speed problem we have, bubba?" He took a long drag and shook his head and said, "I don't know." He exhaled and kind of laughed as he said something about putting his fastest Marines in the squad all in one team. I agreed but was concerned that splitting the teams up would fuck up team cohesion. He snapped back quickly with, "If we can't catch up to them what's the difference? Our job is to close with and destroy them." I agreed and we set the plans in motion.

We would be taking our fastest Marines in the squad and putting them in one team. This would become known as the runner team. In the event that you find and fix the enemy, the runner team explodes out from your position under the cover fire of the remaining two teams. They continue to suppress the enemy with mass firepower as the runners sprint up the field. Once in grenade range, the suppression stops and the teams begin to echelon via travel and overwatch to the runners. When the runners are in grenade range, they toss, stack and clear. I wasn't sure I would ever be in the right situation to use this tactic to a T, but I was ready to if the situation arose. My runners were Charette's team. They already happened to be the fastest guys in the squad. Joey was a squad leader who taught me to always continue to think about the enemy and how to better kill him. He taught me so much and will never know my thanks and gratitude. We lost Joey to cancer a few years after getting home from Marjah. He is, has been and will forever be sorely missed.

Too Far South

A short time after being here at Five Points I was cut loose and began to patrol the area. I was put into the current rotation and was on patrol cycle. I went to the COC and checked in with the watch officer and submitted my patrol route overlay. It would be taken and put up on a tracking board in the COC and we would be tracked in case we needed to be supported by the company assets. The mission for my patrol was to locate and grid out any and all mosques in the area. We needed to start to paint a picture of our battle space and that was an important piece of information to have. Most of the time in the Middle East the imams or religious leaders, like pastors, are a great source. They know their flock, and they know who is not from the area. They can be a great asset or a horrible enemy, able to manipulate the local populace in their stead. LT was with me as we punched out of the north exit of the COP and broke into a staggered column turning north up Route Taunt, a super shady area where there are canals on both sides of the road and the others had been in contact many times. We made a move to the east through a waist-deep wadi and up into a blooming poppy field where we continued for almost another "click" (1000 m) until reaching a small mosque. We recorded all the needed data from the leader of the church and pushed across the street into a small compound that was vacant to take a water break and cool down. It was 100+ degrees that day.

While we were resting LT and I conversed about a strange mosque-looking compound to the south that looked super shady. With LT's blessing I radioed into the COC watch office and requested permission to proceed to the south in order to check this last mosque before returning to base. The watch officer replied that the compound in question was below the 86 northing which was dangerous, and thus the reason for us requesting permission to go. He followed up with, "Permission granted. Make sure you get comms checks every 30 mikes." I looked at LT who was staring at me awaiting the go. I gave him a subtle nod, spoke to the team leaders and we broke down, setting out for the south. We were way opened-up in a staggered column as we made our way into a wadi-filled southern sector that seemed to go from a buzz to a hush as we moved through the area.

We stayed with our dispersion the best we could, but the area had some natural chokepoints that slowed us. When I finally made it to the mosque, I instantly knew that we were going to be hit soon. The atmospherics shifted for the worst as I was communicating with the imam. Cpl. Charette radioed to me that he had seen some dude moving around suspiciously to the south of our position and I should get the hell back out of there. I was next to LT as we began to ease back away from the little church. The imam and his compatriots looked at us with some extreme hate in their eyes. It doesn't take very many days in Marjah before you know what the looks on the MAMs means. They were no more than 25 meters down the road away from the mosque. I radioed to Wetzel to keep his eyes peeled to the south and started to work out of the area.

Instantly the air exploded with small arms and medium machine gunfire that seemed to be all over us. It was a well-planned and well-executed ambush where we were getting engaged from two sides and within less than two minutes, we became fully enveloped. This was a situation that I hadn't been in before and being that it was new to me I was doing my best trying to not let anyone die. I started a counterattack with my men and drove back the enemy that was firing from the front left of the squad. As we rushed the compound with two teams, my third team was out on the flank covering our right side. Cpl. Bennett had dropped a guy or two in the building and we were trying to close to get their weapons when my green gear cracked to life with Captain Biggers. "Hey Stud, what the fuck are you doing south of the 86? We don't go down there with anything less than a platoon. It's a fucking hornet's nest down there!" I was completely confused because I had requested permission to be here and was granted it by the watch officer. I tried to communicate that to the boss but was directed to shut my mouth and break contact from the enemy. I was to get my ass to back to the COP as soon as possible. This completely took the air out of my sails. I started to break back toward my guys when we began to get engaged heavily. Feeling enveloped yet again, I requested immediate smoke from the mortar section. That is a white phosphorous round that burns at over 5000 degrees causing tons of billowing smoke. The problem is that if it happens to land on someone it looks like we tried to maim the enemy which is not allowed. This is where politics and war shouldn't be intertwined. As much as I agree that burning men is a bad thing, losing a single life over a political decision is repulsive. I was denied obscuration smoke from higher and was forced to break contact without it. I directed the squad down into a four-and-a-half-foot deep wadi that ran north for much longer than I would need it.

Being in the wadi we would have cover and concealment but would lack visibility. It was flowing into us as we trudged through. Little Wright was almost lost to the water during this breakback, as the water was over his head in some spots. The rounds were on us so bad that multiple Marines were skinned through their clothing. I remember seeing the fear in some of their eyes as the rounds ripped through the cattails that were now over our heads as we moved through the water. It was a look I hated seeing in any Marine's eyes. Marines don't get that look often. When they do it's always a memorable event.

The further away from the enemy we got the madder I became. I was pissed that we could be granted permission to move south and then get chewed out like that, not to mention denying my requested fires while my Marines were in danger. I suppose maybe they were denying me for reasons outside my control or knowledge, but at the time it felt cold. I remember being told to come see the captain with my LT as soon as we got back, which meant the ass-chewing still wasn't over. We were about 350 meters from where contact was initiated before the enemy started to ease up on the wadi. We continued straight north for what seemed like forever before the point crawled up and out of the wadi. Just south of the bazaar that led back to the wire, I stopped to count the Marines into the bazaar and out of the wadi. I instructed the team leaders to get straight to the hooch and download gear, get my weapon and gear counts and start cleaning rifles. Upon getting back, I would be accompanying Lt. Emmanuel to get chewed out by the captain once more.

Lt. Emmanuel, knowing that I was beyond pissed and borderline insubordinate, instructed me to not say a word while we were in with the CO, even though he was of the same opinion as I was that it was time to choose what battles were smart to fight and which ones to save for another day. In his opinion, this was one to slide on. I disagreed but with respect for him I stayed quiet and took the reaming. The issue for me was that a watch officer decided to clear me hot without checking if that was okay, then rolled over on the PFC on radio watch, saying the PFC must have relayed that information to my squad. But both the LT and I both knew who was on the radio when we were in talks about moving south. It was not the PFC radio watch.

The ass-chewing ended with us being told that our break contact looked bad in the GBOSS and I was to remain grounded to the COP for two weeks retraining my men. It was nothing short of an embarrassment tactic that seemed below the CO himself. At any rate, no more did I come out of that ass-chewing than I was walking back to the berthing and got word on black gear that while in the wadi one of the squad's metal detectors was washed away off the flak of the man carrying it. I stopped dead in my tracks, looked down at my boots and started laughing. I still hadn't taken my gear off, so I grabbed the PTT and told Charette thanks for the heads up. I shook my head and did a crisp about-face in the sand, tracing the C and whipping around. I walked back toward the COC to get another helping of that ass-chewing, as if I hadn't had enough already. Just before opening the tent to go in and make the squad look even better, I hear Gunny Mack asking where I was going now. He was in the familiar "Gunny Lean" we all know, posted up in the shade. He didn't even look up at me as he peered and asked. I replied that one of my Marines lost his metal detector on the route back up north in the wadi. "I'm going to let the CO know, Gunny." I said it in a cheerful tone to which he thought may have sounded like "fuck you," I suppose. He then proceeded to chew my ass for about 10 minutes and sent me in to see the captain again. It was a long day, to say the least. My restriction to the COP wasn't as bad as it was originally set out to be, and the sir and I hashed out our differences in a private conversation one night after he accompanied me on my first patrol out of the wire in a week. With the CO's, blessing everything went back to normal.

Feeling back to normal it was time for the rest of the outcasts to come out from Hanson and lay it on the enemy. I couldn't wait to be operating in full force again, and I really took Staff Sergeant Wright for granted up until then. Until I was without his buffering, I didn't realize how much buffering he would do for us on a regular basis. It was an incredible difference. I would be seeing my platoon in a week and then we would be entering the already-established operation cycle at Five Points.

OP Life

Our rotation once all on deck out at COP Reilly was 10-10-10, meaning 10 days on post cycle at COP Reilly, 10 days on patrol cycle and 10 days on OP duty. Breaking it down like this was a good way to fight the monotony in the grind. Ten days seemed to be a good amount of time to fight before really needing to come back and chill for a bit. It was also the point at which you were ready to go back and fight when you were out at the OP on day nine and 10. It can become very disheartening and tiresome if you're not engaging the mind constantly. Most times on OP rotation you would get a lot of down time because there wasn't always a patrol going out. I would read to pass the time. While in country I read all of Marcus Latrell's "Lone Survivor" while battling boredom and camel spiders in the OPs. Reading his accounts of combat resonated and the thought of journaling my experience became reinforced.

I took the OP cycles very seriously at OP3 where I was assigned. It was a shanty of a compound with camo netting for a roof and a very small hut with a medium-sized rectangular courtyard. There were 2 entries, an entry on the east and an entry on the west side of the courtyard walls where two Marine posts were built up, and then there were two additional ANA posts facing north and south. I was very concerned about killing a specific guy who was trying to lay IEDs frequently in a culvert that was approximately 300 meters from my building. He was a very dedicated and crafty implanter who was already responsible for blowing up a 6x6 tactical vehicle with one of my buddies, Sgt Lewis, in the passenger seat, who was sent north for scans on his head following the incident. I was sent to the OP to make sure it didn't happen again.

Of the first important things to tend to at the OP was placing a trip flare on the culvert and daring this motherfucker to come while I was here. I would also have the Marines build their own fire-plan sketches of the area and reinforce their own posts, as well as supplemental posts in case the need to stand more in defense should ever arise. On the way out to the OP I stopped briefly at the culvert and looked at it. The engineers had already been out and attached some HESCO grating on either end of the tile as to make it more difficult for this guy to place his explosives. It gave me the perfect place to set up my flares. I would return under the cover of darkness to attach the trap. We continued to push through the heat east until we met up with Joey Harms and his squad at the OP. We always took our time during changeover and talked tactics. As the Marines were helping transfer info from his squad to mine, we talked in the radio room of the OP. We talked about implementing our runner teams and turning the heat up on the enemy. He gave me a data dump from the previous 10 days, including non-relevant gripes and moans from peer to peer. It was so hot that we dripped sweat in the nighttime air as we spoke softly over some cold coffee. I couldn't drink hot coffee while it was 100 degrees out and I was already soaked through. Once the changeover was complete, we watched as the squad disappeared into the darkness.

Once the evening settled, I took a small team of Marines down to the culvert and attached a trip flare to the grate and tied the wire in place to trip when the grate was moved in the slightest little bit. We waited and waited. I don't know how many nights it took but he finally fucked up and tipped the flare, earning himself some 5.56 therapy from both me and Cpl. Bennett. He didn't blow anymore Marines up; he just lay dead in an irrigation ditch awaiting his buddies to come wheel him away in a wheelbarrow. I was super satisfied with the kill and slept well that night. Cpl. Bennett shot well.

During one of the OP cycles shortly after this happened, I had a very scary instance come about during the day. We received a call from higher that some of our psychological operation Marines intercepted some traffic that made them believe that the OPs were about to be attacked in force. I was radioed at around 1830 that I needed to be alert all night and "stand two." This means that I stand additional posts up to be more defensive and harder to kill. Thankfully we had already built the shells of the stand two posts, so there wasn't much to do in that respect.

I pulled the boys in and gave them all the information that I was given. They all understood what needed to happen and what was expected of them. I started to take out Claymore mines and had Grimes and Charette assist in the placement. Both the entryways to the courtyard were skinny hallways for three to five feet and then turned directly into the courtyard. I emplaced my mines in the sandbag hallways facing out, camouflaged with an empty green sandbag. If they wanted to come in here and get us, they were going to lose a bunch of men to do it. I ran both clackers to the mines into the makeshift radio room table that was made from our extra MRE boxes.

That night was one of the scariest nights of my life. I didn't sleep at all throughout the entire night. At all times either Charette or myself were manning the clackers and radio. We had already spun up some grid missions for mortars and had prepped everyone's belts with 40 mm grenades for the M203 gunners. When I wasn't in the office, I was walking the posts and keeping the Marines on post vigilant. I would move to each post and talk to my guys for about 35 minutes to an hour. I would ask if they were good to go, and then slip to the next post. It was a long, hot night where everything that made a noise was a potential threat. Or at least that's the way it seemed. As the sun started to break the horizon, I stirred the kindling under the pot of hot water. I was making coffee because to get through the day was going to be a challenge. The entire squad was up all night and we were smoked. It wouldn't be so terrible if you could catch a nap during the day and get ready for the evening again or even patrol, but you couldn't sleep during the daylight hours. You could literally watch the Marines and soldiers who were asleep in the courtyard physically roll toward the east wall in their sleep without waking up to avoid the heat from direct sunlight. Once it was on you, you were up. Until it was gone again you were awake. Never did anyone come for us from any direction that night or any night while at the OPs. I wondered a lot if the interception was referring to another group of friendlies in a similar situation.

Frequently from the OP on a lazy day, one could make lunch and if lucky, observe 1/6 to the south engaged in a gunfight, or you could face the opposite direction and watch our very own Lima Company in the shit. There were many a day out at the OP when we were watching the war like they did so many generations before us. It was always captivating too, to watch the explosions and then the counterattacks. With constant snapping of rounds piercing the air we would cheer on our compatriots with whoops and laughter. Finally, after a bit, the A-10 warthogs would show up. They are an impressive piece of gear. When watching from range you can see the plane slow down in mid-dive as the main gun opens, only you see the impacts of the rounds before you can hear the brrrrrt brrrrrrt from the A-10's main gun. It's truly amazing to have that for your afternoon entertainment.

Once we were at the OP, we observed Lima Company in a fight way to the north of us for most of the morning. After they slipped into what seemed to be a lull, we broke out some lunch and the post standers changed out. Some of the Marines had a hankering to play spades so we made our way into the OP radio room where the makeshift table was located. The deck was shuffled, and the cards were dealt. "First-hand deals itself," I said, as I was organizing all my spades in the left of my hand in descending order, then sequentially organized the other suits. The cards began to fly and we were about mid-way through the set when a deafening roar and scream split the air. We all ducked and held our breath awaiting the death we were certain must be following. I looked up to see an Israeli fixed-wing fast mover bust the sound barrier right over the OP. He was so low to the ground we could see his mask and eyes inside the cockpit. He was called in by Lima who was back at it in a fight for a show of force. A show of force is something that we would use to scare the enemy. They didn't really understand the fast movers or the long-range weapons at all. They would be doing this to the enemy and hopefully dropping ordnance. We all were scared shitless. We didn't talk about it much after it happened, but spades was over for the day, to say the least. And most of us had to clean out our undershorts. Each time we came to the OPs another month had gone by and the deployment started to have a rhythm to it.

While at the OP one time later in the deployment, we had been up all day for a patrol effort. When we got back, everyone was gearing down and because we had Herby and some of the machine gunners on deck, the spades began to fly. SSgt. Wright was also on deck. We all huddled around our makeshift spades table as the sun began to fall completely out of the sky.

The headlamps popped on, and after some housekeeping items being taken care of with the company command, we continued playing. As the cards flew, we could hear little scratching noises occasionally. We were leaned up against the HESCO wall and figured it was some type of critter on the inside that we were hearing. As Herby was calling out what he had on "Little Mo" (a great hand in spades), a giant camel spider skidded down the wall like he was ready to eat some damn body. Herby sort of freaked and grabbed a bigger flashlight to swat the monster with. I don't remember how many times he hit the spider, but I don't recall it dying. The skidder disappeared and we went about clowning on one another for letting the bitch come out the way we all did. No more than two minutes later, we heard a mass of skidding noises and there were a pair of skidders literally running right at us down the walls. Instead of being big bad-ass Marines we all thought there may be some type of demonic possession and we split to the center of the OP. Then, with the enemy drawn out of his comfort zone, we began to stomp their little asses. But it took a solid two minutes for us to regain control of the situation. In the end we ran that Little Mo and then turned in for the evening.

As soon as the sun touched my face I rose up and headed to the hygiene area to wash and brush my teeth and shave. I would always use the two minutes that I brushed my teeth in the morning as my personal "not think about anything" time. I would close my eyes and try to forget about everything if only for a few seconds. Forget about Matthias and Currier, forget about Vuocolo having a hole in his arm, just think about nothing at all. Most times it didn't last but a few seconds, but I cherished those few seconds. Once back to reality I spit the toothpaste out on the sand and took a swig of water to rinse down the rest. I made my way back over to the berthing where I found Herby sitting up on his cot, rubbing the sleep out of his eyes. I looked at him and he said, "Hey asshole, did you fucking burn me in my sleep?" He held up his arm and pointed to a nasty-looking purplish wound on his inside arm at the crotch of his elbow. I was flabbergasted that he would even think that I would burn him, let alone burn him in his sleep, let alone burn him in his sleep without waking him. I laughed and said something like, "Yeah I burned you in your sleep without waking you up Herby...!" We both laughed and surmised that it must have been that spider he failed to end in the beginning of our spades game. He came back for one last revenge bite. Either that or someone burned him in his sleep without waking him. To this day he still wears a scar in the crotch of his arm from the bite/burn.

Patrol Cycle

Patrols initially out in Five Points were super eerie. I suppose it had a lot to do with the area being new. Not knowing the area increases the stress level and focus on patrol by a million times. It's obvious that patrolling in the heat with that heavy of a load is extremely tiring, but what is not so obvious is the mental exhaustion that comes from being overly focused and attentive.

One of my very first times out in the new AO, we were something like halfway through the route when the wind blew, and every single Marine's head snapped crisply all together as if given a facing drill movement. I hit the PTT and told the point to follow his nose. He chuckled and said, "Roger that." He banged a left and took us down into a small wadi crossing. It was super-hot outside and I could feel my skin cooking in the heat as I plopped down into the water at the crossing. I splashed some water on my neck and tried to forget about how dirty it was. It was commonplace to see several people throughout the day pissing or shitting in the canals and wadis. Climbing up the other side, the smell was now stronger and more pronounced. I hadn't smelled such an aroma in several years. We opened again into a tactical column and moved through the fields until we finally happened upon the largest field of marijuana I have personally ever seen. It must have been at least five to 10 acres if not more. The stalks were thick like corn at the bottom and they stood up to four and five feet. The buds on the tops of the plants were sticky and the oozing was so heavy on some that they were bent over from the weight. My corpsman instantly hit his knees and said, "My next wish is a dump truck full of rolling papers." We all laughed and made our way through the rows. We found out later that the weed farmers were not our enemy per se, but they would pop off some rounds toward us if it looked like we were hurting the crops. It was another way the Taliban had control over the people. The pot farmers only got a very small amount of weed for personal use and next to no money. The Taliban would just come in and take their crops.

Patrol cycle was always my favorite time of the month. The thing I enjoyed the least was being so close to the company flagpole. Even though the base came with its amenities it also came with constant working parties and all-around fuckery. Sometimes it would come from 2B, sometimes Gunny Mack, sometimes the 1st Sgt. While on patrol cycle, we would have between one and three patrols in a 24-hour period. They could last anywhere from an hour and a half to six to eight hours, all depending on what took place. For instance, we had once located an IED which we were told to hold a cordon on until EOD arrived. We were relieved from our cordon 11 hours later, the following morning. It was shitty when you ran into a fight on your morning patrol and didn't get back into the wire until it was time to step out on the next one. It didn't happen often, but it happened often enough to talk about. We did have some flex room when things like this came up. We would usually shift the additional patrols to the following evening. Sometimes we had to lace up and shut up, push on and make things work. But that's what grunts do. We embrace the suck.

One afternoon my squad was on patrol cycle and was scheduled for an evening patrol to overwatch a field that was suspected of enemy activity. This usually meant they were coming out at night and digging weapons up to use that night or soon after; or they were digging in weapons to hide them for other enemy fighters. Sometimes they were digging in IEDs as well. At any rate, we would be observing the field and reacting to the enemy activity that could present itself. It was sometime around 1300 when I finished my bullshit workout in the gym, and I was walking back to the berthing when the radio chirped with the COC needing me at the tent.

When I reported in to the COC they were tracking two individuals on the GBOSS making their way north on Route Taunt, one of the five roads that intersected at the bazaar outside our base. They were carrying what appeared to be 82 mm mortars, and possibly RPGs. I was tasked to track them down and kill or capture them, depending on the situation. The evening patrol was scrapped, and I radioed Charette to get the squad moving and to lace up for a fight. He could tell from the tone of my voice that it was not time to fuck around. In less than two minutes the squad was pushing out the main entry control point (ECP) and into the bazaar. I briefed them on the move. The compound in question was only 600 meters to the north straight up Taunt. We needed to be careful, though. Taunt was flanked on the left side by a deep canal. This was not a good idea to walk up so we broke off Taunt on the east side and moved in a wedge formation with my newly established "fast team" in point. I was in the middle of the wedge just behind the point team and flanked by the other two teams. The plan was simply to contact the occupants of the target building and do a simple search for the weapons. If they were Taliban, we would know it quickly by the way they acted, especially if they opened up on us during entry. As the thought raced through my mind I decided to radio back for an update. They were keeping an eye out for me with the GBOSS, and they did indeed have an update for me. They said that the two MAMs appeared to drop off the ordnance in the south end of the compound, in a small room with a small blue door. They didn't see them emerge yet from that door.

As the squad closed, I ordered 3rd Team with Grimes at the helm to close and hold a near-side cordon on the southeast corner of the courtyard. I was now moving up with the point team behind Wetzel. Bennett's team under the control of Knuckles would be holding rear security and roll in for reinforcements if needed. If not needed, they would still roll into the building upon it being secured, and they would move straight to the roof to pop overwatch. At that point in the push, they even made it look sexy.

That small storage room with the blue door was now in my sights as we moved through 3rd Team's cordon. We stacked on the door briefly and made entry. After a short clear out it was obvious there was no one in the room; they had slipped out before we got there. We also saw no weapons or ammo. "Room clear!" one Marine said as we exited the small room and now made our way to the main side of the building. It was a nice courtyard with a bunch of vines and trees, way nicer than the other set-ups in the area, and way harder to clear as well.

The squad infilled nice and smooth, immediately clearing their corners and picking up the danger areas that appeared and calling out to the locals that were filing out of the huts.

"Hands! Hands! Hands! Get 'em up."

"Down on your knees."

There was a total of three males and two females. The squad separated the MAMs from the elderly man, and they sent the women inside the main hut once cleared. Third Team was rolling to the roof as I made my way over to the military-aged males. I called in the description to higher and had Charette get them on their knees. I left him there and moved over to investigate the elderly man. He was someone who I can truly say made me feel like he was dangerous. He creeped me out, he had the same eyes as the crazy guys from the beginning of the push, the crazy guys that always attacked us. I questioned the old man about the boys' whereabouts and his general distain for me. He spat at me and said, "The Taliban run the country better than the United States." When John, my interpreter, translated it to me, I radioed him in as suspicious and asked the command if I could detain him for further questioning by our human intel specialists.

He had already had multiple IEDs emplaced outside his compound and now what appeared to be ordnance of some type being transported. They agreed and I took the old man under my control. He was not thrilled about it, but worse, the MAMs lost their shit completely, becoming enraged that I zip-tied his hands behind his back, placed a pair of blackout goggles on him and placed him on his knees. I wanted to bring the boys in as well, but the command would not authorize me to do that. We kept them on their knees as we did an in-depth search of the area and the huts. We found tons of batteries, mainly D batteries, and copper wiring. We found pictures on the inner walls of the compound depicting stick figures shooting down US helicopters with RGPs. This became commonplace to see in this area. After I was satisfied that we had searched enough, I logged all the pertinent information and prepared to exit the compound with the old man in tow. I briefed the squad that we needed to move smartly back to the base because they were surely going to be pissed we took the old man, especially if they were Taliban. I told them I would be running the old man with me and we would be pushing the pace until back at the bazaar, in case we got ambushed. The instructions were clear as we broke out of the compound on Route Taunt. My goal was to move quickly down Taunt until we established contact and then travel and overwatch back to the bazaar, something we became great at in the months out at Five Points. The enemy out there was notorious about hitting you from behind as you began your return to base (RTB). Most of the time they were being managed and controlled by the commander from a phone or walkie-talkie.

Rounds were cracking all over the place as I ran the old man through the flooded field. We had only made it south down Taunt about 250 meters before the air was split open by small arms. I could only assume that the boys had weapons in a nearby compound and grabbed them up as we made our way out. The more they fired, the more pissed off I became. They weren't shooting at me; they were shooting at my boys. They wouldn't want to hurt this old man, I thought. As the rounds snapped by my head too close for comfort I started to wonder if instead they were trying to kill him. Maybe he had information they didn't want us to have. Whatever the case, we continued to move as my squad kept up the fight with the enemy. It was horrible running a person through a gunfight blindfolded. He endured more pain than he otherwise would have, had they not fired at us.

Once back at the bazaar the MAMs gave it up and retreated, it seemed. We had an additional squad waiting for us in case we needed help. As we moved through them smiles and shouts were exchanged. The gunfight was through but some of the Marines were still buzzing. I turned at the ECP and dropped to a knee. I put the old man on his knees beside me and counted my guys into the wire. Coming in last I told the TLs to get the weapons and gear cleaned and get chow in the boys. I split from them with a bump of the Kevlars as if we were "pounding the rock" and headed with the old man to the mini detention facility (DETFAC). Once I transition the authority of the detainee to the DETFAC, I'm through with him. I have no further responsibility. I only say that because after that night I am not sure what happened to the old man. He was taken away to be interviewed and I didn't hear anything else.

I assumed they moved him up to the main DETFAC located at Camp Hanson, where V was sent to work as a consequence of his shoulder wound. Once the old man got in there it's hard to say what happened. I know I never saw him in the AO again, though. However, just outside the same house was a hot spot for the duration while we were there. On one occasion outside that house, there were two men identified on the GBOSS digging an IED into the ground. They were smooth about parking their motorbike sideways in the road for obscuration. One acted as a lookout as the other was on his hands and knees with a tarp over him connecting the wires and finishing the dig. The GBOSS offered an elevated view, projected onto an 80-inch LG flat-screen monitor located in the COC.

I was just out of the shower walking back to my berthing when I ran into Harms at the smoke pit. He was burning one with some of his guys. I stopped to have a Newport and chat with him a minute. I loved a Newport directly following brushing my teeth; it enhanced the flavor or something. I still had shaving cream on my earlobe and lower neck as I claimed a sandbag off the wall. Taking the towel off my shoulder I wiped the remnants away and wrapped the towel up tight around my neck. Harms had a burning desire in his eyes when he said he had implemented and been successful with his runner teams. We spoke in depth before deciding to move our conversation into one of the air-conditioned hooches. On my way to the berthing my black gear chirped with the CO who needed me at the COC. Harms smiled, winked and said, "Get some, Rogers! Holler at me when you're back." I guess he could tell by the tone of the voice on the other end of the radio that this was going to be a real one.

Swiping open the flap to the COC was always refreshing because of the polar air that you were met with, sending instant chills up my spine. Following that was the sweet aroma of freshly brewed coffee. Any worth-a-shit Marine COC always has fresh coffee, hot and ready to go. As I shuffled in, I filled up a small Styrofoam cup and moved to the viewing area. Everyone was huddled around the flat screen. There were two MAMs that had ridden up on a moped and abruptly stopped, parked sideways in the road and got off the bike. When I walked in the watch officer was in talks with regiment about drone capabilities and what we could have on station to assist. The CO walked up to me and told me that he was trying to get ISR but in case he couldn't, I needed to go handle this situation.

I watched briefly as the two men were digging the bomb into the earth. I radioed the boys, "Meet me with my gear at the ECP, we're moving on two MAMs on Taunt." Charrette copied and I ducked back out of the polar temps into the hell I loved to hate. I was moving quickly down to the ECP where I met up with Charrette. I laced up and prepared to push out when the CO radioed me to get to the COC double time. When I walked back in, this time fully dressed for battle, they again were all surrounding the TV. Someone said that they had gotten a predator in the sky armed with Hellfire rockets. I chuckled and awaited the show. With everyone completely tuned in, the two men continued their work, not knowing what was happening now or what was about to happen in a minute. The intensity grew almost unbearable in the COC awaiting the ordnance. Finally, with a quick flash, the two men were blown away. When I say blown away, literally they were blown away: one into a wadi on the flank of Taunt and the other into a nearby ditch. The two men must have heard the rocket ignite as it dropped off the wing of the predator, because in the video just before the explosion they both stood and turned to one another as if to run away but they didn't make it far. The CO gave me the nod and it was simply a BDA (battle damage assessment) mission, and a confirmation that the IED sympathetically detonated.

Working out of the bazaar in a tactical column, we were only a 10-minute walk or so from the scene of the incident. The COC watched as the Taliban came out with wheelbarrows and scooped up the remains of the man who lay lifeless in the ditch. They relayed real-time information to me as it was happening, which as a squad leader in this kind of environment was welcomed and amazing. When the GBOSS and other ISR assets were used for what they were designed for, they worked second to none. When we arrived on the scene there wasn't much of a mess. I expected more blood for some reason. There was none. The man that was blown into the wadi was blown completely out of his button-up manjams. I found the shirt not far from the wadi's edge, very near where he was pulled out from. As the boys scouted around the water's edge, I went through the shirt and found a laminated card in one of the shirt's breast pockets. I noticed the writing was in Pashtun (the native language in the area) on one side of the card and something different on the other side. I collected the card for the intel guys, putting it into a plastic sensitive sight exploitation (SSE) bag. I marked the date and time and other required fields on the data card and stuffed it into my front pouch on my plate carrier. There would be a bunch more information to go with the kit before turnover, but that was stuff I could fill out when time was less sensitive.

Unfortunately, the IED appeared to have not sympathetically detonated with the rocket strike. I was impressed. Our EOD bubbas were rolling with us and we set up a nearside cordon for them. They would move up and mitigate the threat while the squad held security. Sometimes you would hold for two hours and sometimes 22 hours. In Marjah the longest I had to wait was 11 hours. It was in the early days at Hanson when IEDs were being found at the cyclic rate. We held for a while before the black gear cracked and the charges were set. Due to the terrain with the wadi on one side of the road and sparse cover and concealment, we had to hold our security from an unsafe distance from the controlled detonation.

When the blast ripped through the air it was punishing. As Marines we enjoy the rush and everyone cheers and whoops at the danger, but also it's a way of dealing with fear and negative emotions. We all knew we were too close to that detonation, but sometimes you're not left with perfect scenarios with unlimited resources to choose from. Sometimes risking the blast is more important to ensure you are properly covering your buddies six. That why the Marines are the greatest fighting force the world has ever seen; because in a moment's notice, they will risk absolutely everything, to their final breath, to protect the Marines to their left and to their right. With the IED threat neutralized and the eardrums ringing, we began to travel and overwatch our way back towards the bazaar. We would return with the intel bag and the little remaining materials that the EOD team picked up. I met up with the company intel rep and handed over the SSE bag with the laminated card and briefed him on what I encountered at the site. After a few minutes we were through, and I went to offload my gear. The squad was already cleaning weapons and getting chow. We would still be on react and you never knew when you would be heading out. We were slated for a late-night patrol though, so most of the boys bedded down.

I took the time to head to the showers and wash off the day. I downloaded my kit in the berthing and grabbed a bar of Irish Spring soap that I got in a package from one of my relatives. Flip-flops on and a washcloth and towel, and I was on my way. I let Charette know where I was going and left the comms with him. Grabbing my M4 from the rack, I stood up and made my way to the shower bays. There was a small area to put your weapon and then a huge pallet of water already warmed from the heat of the sun. I grabbed four or five bottles and began to fill up the water bag for the bag shower that hung slightly above head-height in a makeshift wooden shower house. It was nice but as one would imagine it had stayed wet and nasty from overuse. I always felt like no matter what the day threw at me, I could wash it away with a shower and a good night of sleep. Following the shower, I moved to the 82 mm gun pit to see if anything was going on. With an empty gun pit I moved to the regular smoke pit and found Herby and Harms bullshitting. I joined and bummed a Newport off Herby. Sitting on the sandbags, we looked up at the stars and talked about what we would do if we hit the lottery, or whether aliens were real. Sometimes shit could go way deep in the smoke pit. If Grimes was present in the pits, he would constantly troll others, usually with a comment like "God is fake, you idiots" or something along those lines. Everyone would begin getting cranky and he would ultimately get the last laugh. The day was good.

Roads and Runners

Tyler Roads was a radio operator who was attached to the company. He was a good-looking kid, tall, with a good build and thick dark hair. He didn't look like your average "rock-biting" comm Marine. He stood 6 foot 2 or so, with an athletic build. He was the personal comms guy for the higher headquarters. He was always on the COP manning the radios and coordinating with higher. He would often be found running and working out, listening to tunes, and most surprisingly, probing for more information about the infantry. He would always stop me and ask me tactical questions; not to suck up or get in good with someone in a brown-nosing way, but with what seemed to be a genuine want for the answers. I remember several occasions when he had asked me to take him out on patrol with us. I always laughed at him, shaking my head knowing that the CO would never sign off on it. He would have been an amazing asset and he wanted to go outside the wire and get some, and I liked that about Roads. I would always tell him that if the CO said it was straight, I was good with it, never thinking that it would happen.

Usually when the squad would come back in the wire after a gunfight Roads was among the first people at my cot ready to hear the debrief; if he wasn't on shift, that is. It was like he was living vicariously through me and the boys. I am certain my squad was not the only squad he did this with, but we really liked having him around. We would trade the stories of the day for good intel from the Headquarters , as he was always around the CO and more importantly the CO's radios. We frequently ate chow together and worked out at the gym. He was not great at spades but had his good days. He was the most grunt-like POG I had ever met. Even down to his operating gear, he was a grunt at heart. His gear was neatly set up the same as our squad. He was a total gear bomb, but it sure made his shit look tight. He had all Blackhawk aftermarket pouches, and everything was set up for field-expedient comms use.

One day after noon chow, Roads busted into my berthing to find me in my bag trying to catch some sleep before the next patrol. He slapped my leg and said, "Take me out this afternoon with y'all." I told him he knew the CO wouldn't have it. He said, "I already talked to him and said he was good with it." I confirmed with the COC and then smiled and said, "Okay Roads, let's pop that combat cherry, be outside my hooch at 1445 laced up ready for PCCs and PCIs."

The expression that came across this young Marine's face was that of sheer bliss and euphoria. Seeing that pride and eager willingness to take the fight to the enemy with his brothers in the name of the United States of America gave me cold chills. It takes a special person to be in his position, secluded inside the wire, or on trucks, wanting and begging to fight the enemy. It fueled and motivated me. He turned from elated to serious after he checked his watch, and he ran out to get his gear together and clean his gun.

I was so energized by his joy that I couldn't get back to sleep, and I only had about two hours before I needed to start moving anyway. I wiped the sleep from my eyes and sat up. I slipped my Danner Jungle boots on leaving them unlaced. I pulled my boot bands off the laces and tucked my FROG bottoms underneath and dropped the blouse all the way to my ankle, the way it was meant to be worn. Pulling on my FROG top, I stood and grabbed my M4 from inside my sleeping bag and walked to the exit of my hooch with my toothbrush. After I brushed my teeth and washed up, I walked up to the COC to arrange my "on call" targets for patrol, draw up my intended patrol route and check on supporting agencies.

It looked like the company JUMP trucks would be on a convoy just south of my patrol. They were a four- to five-truck element with turret-mounted 240s, a 50-caliber M2, and an MK19 fully automatic grenade-launching machine gun. That's a good bit of firepower should we need some help. I linked up with the JUMP section leader, a short corporal confident and competent in his abilities, and informed him of where I would be located and told him to be listening for us, as the past few visits to the sector we were in pretty good fights. He said, "I got ya covered, bubba." And we parted ways.

After I finished my chores, I went to the back of the COC to see Captain Biggers. He had his personal berthing in the back of the command center constructed out of wood, with a small cot like we slept on and very few comfort items. Everything was in its place and tidy as one would expect. I wanted to see him to ensure I was cleared to take Roads out with me face-to-face. I knocked on the door and he ushered me inside. We had a brief chat about what was expected. It was a short conversation in which he simply smiled and said, "Don't let Roads get killed, Rogers!" I said, "Roger that, sir." I gave a head nod to the 'sir' and headed back to my berthing. With the squad stirring for patrol, I sat on my cot and studied the area we were headed to. I called over Wetzel and covered the bridges I wanted to use and the compound I wanted to set up on at the midway point of the patrol. He took my instructions and then formulated a route. He had become an excellent point man throughout the push and was at a stage where he didn't need to be micromanaged at all. If on-the-spot changes needed to be made, we utilized the black gear and made the adjustment. He had come a long way since the day we dropped in.

At 1440 I walked out of my hooch to conduct PCCs and PCIs and found the entire squad standing by for me, already inspected by the TLs. I threw my kit on and proceeded to the first man in the line, LCpl. Roads, grinning from ear to ear. I checked him over and could feel the energy and excitement pouring out of him. He couldn't stop smiling the whole time I looked his gear over. He was ready. I asked him some mission-oriented questions about what to do if A, B and C happens and he answered all correctly. I spot-checked the rest of the Marines knowing that my TLs had already been over each man and fixed his discrepancies if any. With the squad ready to step we conducted COMM checks with the COC, and then I requested to depart friendly lines to kill the enemy.

The watch officer laughed a bit and cleared me to push out the east entrance into the bazaar. We would be going on patrol to the north on intel that a fight awaited. There was some suspicious activity flaring up to the north where the Taliban had noticed and taken advantage of a small bubble of land between our northern line of the AO and the British troops to the north's southern line. Because of the amount of traffic, it was required to deconflict troop movements; we didn't push the line ever. There was talk about moving up in a combined operation with the Brits, but that had to wait for another day we would be patrolling a sector just south of that bubble.

I had been here before; the rooftops were unique for the area. They were not flat roofs like every other roof, they were domed. Each compound had three to four half-moon-shaped domes on top which weren't ideal for cover in a gunfight, but they were better than the compounds with no roofs, or flat roofs. The domes were 24 to 36 inches of hard-packed mud, just like the huts themselves, making them damn near bullet- and rocket-proof; damn near. As we moved out into the bazaar once more to dance with the devil, the mood was calm and atmospherics normal. I always told Roads to stay right beside me unless told otherwise by a TL or myself. As we patrolled out of the market we opened way up into a staggered column and proceeded on. We had about a three-click movement to the OP compound and then from there, we would observe the area for a bit before taking a route north and west back to the COP. Easy day.

The entire way Roads was locked in, listening to everything that I was telling him and looking like a smooth operator. The only thing was, he was nervous. The smiles were gone, and he was on edge. I kept cracking jokes to chill him down, and after a while he seemed to settle in. As we moved through the poppy fields, which were now chiseled, we were closing on a small village with 15 or so compounds interconnected and somewhat spread out. It had been a trouble area before because we used a bad crossing that created a bit of a chokepoint on the squad. Going off that lesson I split out a satellite patrol with Charette's team to make that same crossing, and the rest of the squad continued a few hundred meters further down the canal to a separate crossing. Both elements were mutually supporting this way, and when one team is jammed the other can provide relief instead of being in the jam with them. The runners had less distance to cover so Charette held on the near side of the canal awaiting my element to make it to our crossing. Right at the canals there was always some sort of vegetation to use for concealment, like the cattails that concealed us down south in the canal months earlier. He tucked in tight with his team and began to observe and report activity. There was nothing really off the baseline and soon I had reached my crossing. We crossed together by echeloning in pairs and then reconstituted our formation to carry on. It was smooth.

Just out of sight from our OP compound the atmospherics began to change. Women and children were no longer out, and you could feel the cold eyes of hate and death upon you. I radioed to everyone to stay alert as if they were not already tracking and the once-relaxed 20-year-old boys that composed my squad postured up like the lions that they were, and the mood and tone shifted. It was always an eerie feeling knowing that the enemy was watching you, but you had to get used to it. Continuing, we finally reached the OP. The point team conducted a near-side cordon and Team Two made entry to clear the house. I chose this house because it had been abandoned in the push and no one had moved back into yet. Knowing that it was empty previously, I thought it better to not have to scare locals or remove a family, even if only temporary.

In a counter-insurgency operation, it's important to not fuck that up and create more potential enemies in the process. Kind of a double-edged sword. (You are here to help but in helping you hurt some. The some that you hurt turn against you or at least empathize with the enemy in a stronger way.) Not to mention the compound gave a great unobstructed view of a crossing we wanted to watch, a crossing we had been in a fight at before. Team 3 quickly moved in behind Team 2 and popped to the roof for overwatch. As the Marines secured the area from above, I popped my top and got a sip of water from my camelback. I told Roads to stay ground level and report to me any significant info from the BN tac. He countered wanting to come to the roof, but I told him no, we wouldn't be here very long, and it was an unnecessary risk. He gave up the fight fast and started to mingle with the Charette's team, and I headed up.

Once topside I met up with Grimes who was manning the SAW on the northwest corner. I knelt and pulled out two Newports, lit them both and handed him one. We both took a long drag and exhaled the smoke into the equally hot air. "What do we got?" I asked. He never came out of his scope and replied, "Sweaty balls, hemorrhoids, and bad guys, Sergeant." I laughed and tapped him on the shoulder and said, "Stay frosty." He didn't think the pun was funny. I moved over to the next dome beside Grimes on the roof and glassed a while. Checking out the area through my 4X RCO on top of my weapon. I always found it fascinating to watch a completely different culture go about their daily lives, as if we weren't having a war in their backyards. But, I guess, what else can you do in that position? Goes to show the resiliency of human beings.

After about an hour we hadn't seen anything suspicious other than the atmospheric change and I gave the order to roll it up. The TLs moved into action getting the Marines where they needed to be to punch out once more. At this point the Taliban were notorious for hitting us when we were leaving an area, giving them distance and surprise. Knowing that to be the enemy's current TTP, we were just as cautious leaving as we were when we arrived. Roads and I exited somewhere behind Team 2 knowing that the most likely point of friction would be to the rear. With Grimes's team behind me and Teams 1 and 2 in front we moved in a staggered column with 30 meters' dispersion. We would open bigger once back past the small village and into the poppy fields. Wetzel, at point, led the squad almost reaching the first of many compounds to the front when hell broke loose from a tree line to our back-right flank. Instantly the squad went into action conducting our SOP for a far ambush to the rear. Team 3 dropped in place and laid down a wall of fire. Team 2 made its way to our flank and my runners instantly moved to the compound near to the front and popped to the roof. With an overwatch team in place the fight raged on. The enemy was firing from an east-west running tree line to the north near the bubble previously mentioned. With the pressure relieved from Charette's team, the enemy shut off and seemed to be trying to move to the north undetected to screen the runners. I thought in my mind they were trying to split me and Charette's element which was smart. It would have created problems with our geometries of fire. I called over telling Charrette to lob some 40 mm to the north to interdict the enemy's path and maintain fire superiority as my element was pushing to him.

Following that order his team opened with a hellacious display of firepower where they downed one fighter and had others pinned in a compound. As my element echeloned across the open field to link up, they laid on the triggers keeping the enemy fixed. In just a minute or so I was topside with Charrette and getting oriented with the situation. The field fell silent and we awaited movement. Maybe they were called off or bugged out after they lost some guys, I thought.

It was a perfect time to utilize the runners, but if they were done, we wouldn't have to. After a few minutes Charette's team was replaced by Team 1 and they prepared to run if the fight resumed. They would have to move fast, straight to the north; a drainage ditch essentially ran from our compound 300 meters north to the enemy compound. Once on top of the building the TL would make the decision to frag the compound or not and then make entry to do the cleanup. I called Roads to come up to the roof to show him the battlefield. He would be better oriented this way if he needed to call in for air or other support, should we be engaged again.

He climbed to the roof and posted up right beside me on the same dome. He left his big radio on the roof as to hide the antennas and not draw in a sniper round. As we glassed, I could feel the fight coming back. I told Charette to stay ready down at the exit. Instantly the domed roof we were laying on began to explode in front of us as the enemy ran a burst up, right on target. The rounds must have split us. I took aim and fired as did the overwatch team. Roads, upon receiving contact, lunged back, almost falling off the roof. I grabbed his rig and pulled him down to cover. Smiling, I told him to call in a TIC to the company and give them a POSREP and a SITREP. Stuttering and fumbling over his words he asked, "How do you guys stay so calm?" Everyone that heard him laughed and continued to lay into the enemy. Roads composed his emotion and began to report to higher. At the same time, I launched the runners and increased the rate of fire on the roof. We needed to cover them good until in frag range. As the runners were moving Cpl. Mutter cracked over the comms asking if I was good. I responded with, "Who's on the MK19?" Upon hearing that it was Longshore I was elated. I called Charette and changed the plan up. He took up an advantageous position to the right flank of the enemy 200 meters out in a ditch. I popped yellow smoke on the roof of my building and requested fires from the gun trucks. Before long, the yellow smoke was billowing and I could hear Charette's team taking shots, as they had eyes on the enemy. They continued to push up the wadi, at which point I left Knuckles' team in place on the roof and left to link up with Charette. Upon link-up we stacked up for entry, and Charette held up his frag. I gave a head nod and he prepped to throw. Just before tossing his grenade he heard children inside the compound.

Tucking his frag away we made entry. We found multiple firing positions with expended shell casings and linkage. The enemy had bugged out, but the runner team had been successful. We RTB and encountered no resistance in the process. With Roads safe and back in the wire, I felt like the CO might not want to kill me. I finished my debrief and hit the shower. I met with Harms in his hooch afterward and discussed the day's events and how I used the runners. We talked late into the night about how to better kill the enemy before turning in.

FRAGO

Throughout my entire career as an infantryman, I have always been taught that the "on-scene" commander is the point of contact when things go hairy: refer to the judgment of the man on the ground in the fight. We had been in country awhile and the squad was slated for an evening patrol. Everything was squared away and the patrol's mission was to overwatch and observe a field just north of the COP a click or so. The field was an easy target with plenty of open abandoned compounds to choose from to set up. We knew the enemy had started to count our numbers when we were exiting the COP as the ICOM chatter Marines had intercepted some traffic weeks prior. Many of the squads started having other squads depart with them to have massive numbers; then when they stopped for a break to observe for a bit the additional squad would continue out and back to base. This left an obscured squad behind to watch and kill the enemy. We wouldn't have that luxury this patrol. It was many times difficult to find a willing squad even available, we were so spread thin.

That evening we decided to wait until it was completely dark to step. We wanted the element of surprise. Once outside the wire we worked our patrol north up Summerset and moved through the rather dark and quiet villages. Occasionally someone would be out tending to a cow or goats but most of the time they were inside after dark. As we moved through the small villages I often wondered if the people even knew we were there. Sometimes we were able to move through silently. I couldn't imagine my family having to live like this, I thought to myself. The last stretch to the OP compound I selected was about a click through a chiseled poppy field. Moving through a plowed field is no small task. I hated it. There is nothing like trying to run and fight in them with the loose soil that slips with every step, covered by a thin layer of moondust-like sand.

In the early days at Hanson, LT and I were in the CP talking about counts and we were alerted that one of our sister OPs from another company was hit by small arms. We had trucks at the time and my guys were on react. We mounted up in the MATVs and hauled serious ass. Arriving on the scene we were flanked by canals. We jumped out and the squad started across a chiseled field. When shots started popping off LT took point and started closing on the enemy across the field. I ran as hard and as fast as I could run to echelon with LT but he was lightning-fast. I couldn't ever seem to get sure footing. As badly as I hated the fields, I got over it. The fields were better for dispersion and had far fewer chokepoints to navigate. It was worth the minor pain.

Before long Charette was on the PTT and let me know that we were 200 meters out. His team would run the cordon and the follow-on teams would enter, clear and pop to the roof. Once inside I popped my top and found some steps to sit on. I reached into my drop/chow pouch to retrieve some Jolly Ranchers and an orange Rip It. I would throw one in there before patrol and it would stay cold a while. It was still cold when I cracked it open, and I took a big swig. It was a delicious boost of energy. I crushed the can and threw it back in my drop pouch, pulled a Newport from my shoulder pocket and lit it, inhaling deeply. I took off my gloves and wiped my face with my index finger, flicking away the sweat. Taking another deep draw, I stood, cracked my neck and mused at the stars. You could see so many stars on a clear night here. In overwatch everything is peaceful until it's not anymore. This night was clear; the stars were out, and all was silent. You could hear the occasional goat *bahh* and donkey cry but all was silent otherwise.

After about 30 minutes I laced back up and moved to the roof to check on the boys and glass a bit. We would do this often. Sit on top a roof and watch the local populace go about their daily lives. It always felt surreal to me. I couldn't imagine my family dealing with that like it was normal. But that is why we fight. We watched a while and had no motion in the fields. On my command the squad rolled it up and we departed to return to base. It was a good night, a good patrol.

A click out from the bazaar the green gear squawked. It was the CO requesting to talk to me. I called a short security halt and all the boys laid out holding their respective fields of fire and awaited further orders. I met with Charette and got on the hook.

"Hey stud, listen up; we have some bad dudes with some big guns we need a better eye on. Make your way to this grid and get eyes on the suspected enemy."

"Roger over," I replied, while copying down the grid location. I brought in the team leaders and drew up a plan and a route. The suspected building was well off the main road in the wide-open space. Addressing the map, there was a small drainage ditch that ran up to the MSR. It was flanked by a small cluster of shops. We would slip up that ditch and observe the compound from a distance before making further plans. Before I could even get the squad back on its feet the CO came back on the comms informing me that he was sending out another squad to assist should we need them. The TLs went to each of their guys and informed them of the plan and gave me the ready when all were informed. I gave the signal and the squad rose up like killers in the night and started toward the enemy. I moved with the point team to ditch and then stopped to count everyone. Once my numbers were up, I started to stalk up the ditch between the boys to make it to the front. Charette came over the hook, "Sgt. Rogers, I need you up front now, you wanna see this."

We were nice and spread out, so I took a few minutes getting to the front. As I passed Sadiqu and Wundi Gol, I smiled and said, "Be right back."

At the front of the ditch Charette was in the prone position in good defilade observing the building with mini-thermals. I took the lanyard off his neck and he passed it to me slowly. "Just above the poppy stems on the front corner, see him? Now follow him up to the roof, there are two up there and another one on the back corner. See them?" All the while I was following the directions he was giving. "I do see them."

Through the thermals I could see five armed men, each with a weapon. The two on top of the roof had a long rifle and a machine gun, and the corner posts seemed to have a small arm variant of the AK47. I grabbed the hook and radioed to JT. I explained the situation to both JT and the COC, and JT's squad started my direction. While awaiting them to arrive I started to generate an 81 mm mortar grid mission. I had used both polar and shift missions so far and was about to have the grid mission locked up. I was in awe that they would come set up in our backyard like this. Hell, close enough to be discovered by the GBOSS.

After fifteen minutes the tail end of my squad started to link up with our support, coming up the canal from the rear. I radioed JT, the support squad leader, and asked if he could hard-point a few houses up the road and light the enemy up with infrared lasers. With JT's squad in place, I began reporting to the COC the situation.

The call was mine to make; I could approach the building and clear it out with our small arms, or I could call a mortar mission and level it without risking a single Marine. I chose the latter. I explained to my squad what was happening and started to spin up a mortar mission. Just before I called in the mission, Wundi Guall crawled up and said, "Sergeant Rogers. This no good. Eh, this good security." "Wundi, what the fuck are you talking about? John, get up here," I whispered. When John the interpreter arrived, I got the story. Wundi believed that the enemy were, in fact, host nation security. Good guys! This was not good. I had to call this up to the COC. This was a complete moral issue for me, I didn't want to kill the wrong people. I awaited the command's response. There was a bit of back and forth, because the men did not check into the battle space or get permission from the command about posting up there.

It boiled down to me advancing through the open to make contact with these unknown armed men, and then acting according to the group's identity. I didn't like the Command's idea but sometimes you have to lace up and shut up. I had my mission and my end state.

I was to act and close on the compound to establish contact and verify identity. Not knowing how many men were inside and having to close on the building in the wide-open desert was not ideal; not to mention the fact that there was a sniper and a machine gun on the roof. I decided I would take one team reinforced. Myself, along with Charette's team, would assault, leaving my other two teams at a staging location ready to come to us when needed. My intent was damage control. I wanted to know that when they opened up on us that I still had men to carry on the fight.

To complicate matters, the COC was trying to fight the battle from the GBOSS. They were constantly breaking in on the net to inform me that I needed to push and that the enemy posture was weak. From my vantage point it looked like a trained unit of fighters waiting for some Marines to ambush. After the third remark from the COC about the posture of the enemy I told them that I would handle it from here and turned my comms off. I didn't need them having a "good idea attack" while I was closing with the enemy and out my position.

My one warm and fuzzy thought as we stepped off and broke into a slow, silent stalk through the night was that when this all went south, I could take comfort knowing that all the enemy were going to die. Between JT's squad and the mortar mission I previously worked up, it would be over in a matter of seconds. One loud couple of seconds and they would all perish. I had never, to that point in my life, been more scared to die. I just knew that any second we would be seen, and they would open fire. As we made our approach, it looked like something out of a video game. Through the night optic devices (NVD) everything was green, including the 15 infrared lasers that were shining from across the street and laying on the head of every possible threat in sight. If one shot was fired at me, 100 would be returned. Closing in on the compound I remember distinctly going over range estimation in my head. The only thing I could hear other than my own heartbeat in my eyeballs was the soft-stepping Marines to my right and left. As we closed, I thought about the things I was taught and the lessons I had learned. I was at 150 when I could make out the facial features; now I was at 100 meters. We were spread out in an echelon right formation. I was trying to keep my nerves and breathing in check as we closed close enough to see their eyes. John was instructed to stay right beside me and repeat everything I said. I raised my weapon to find them all fast asleep on their buttstocks.

It was then or never, so I picked up the pace and each man followed. Even if they were friendly forces, being woken up like this could prove fatal. We pushed hard up an embankment made of dried-out poppy stems. I rolled the first man clean off the post where he lay asleep with a firm muzzle thump to the face, grabbing his weapon, and tossing it to the ground, my interpreter by my side repeating every word.

"Hands! Hands! Let me see your hands!" I said as we entered and began to sweep the compound. There were men and weapons everywhere. Within minutes we had the entire compound cleared and we had 26 men and 42 weapons in our control. The guy that got muzzle-thumped was in the corner laying still as I had further talk with the leader of the outfit. The men and weapons all checked out. They were, indeed, a host nation contract security element, who were setting up in the building to protect a "jingle truck" convoy of goods entering Marjah. Because they forgot to check in with the COC, they came very close to losing their lives that night. They are alive only because of my Afghani counterpart Wundi. He knew enough about the area to know what we couldn't. Thank God he stepped up that night.

Up North Census Op

As we closed on the sector we were to "meander about smartly" until contact was established. It was still dark. My skin was wet with the humidity and the sun didn't come up for another 30 minutes. I radioed to Wetzel to set a cordon on the next compound and we would be behind him to make entry and take it down. Here, would take the last break before putting in serious work. As the squad made entry silently everything was smooth. Team 3 popped the roof and posted security, while 1st and 2nd sorted out the occupants. I moved to a small void in the wall and posted up scanning the sector. I was still hot-headed about how the mission brief went in the COC with SSgt. Wright.

Twenty-four hours prior, I was called up to the COC to go over the next day's mission with SSgt. and LT. I told Charette and Wetzel to come along so point could get the route plan started and Charette could get radio frequencies and on-call targets established. Charette could have efficiently taken the squad no doubt on his own at this point, should something happen to me. We met outside my hooch and walked to the command operations center to get the brief. After a down-and-dirty ops plan from LT we broke. SSgt. and I went over to the side and started hashing out the loadouts per squad. It was going to be a hard hit on an entire sector where we had been experiencing a lot of resistance. The plan was to get in the sector early, before sunrise, and then saturate the area until contact was established. The reason I got salty is because that's not how the plan was briefed to me by 2Bravo. He told me to take my squad out and meander about smartly as bait until we established contact with the enemy. He also advised me that he would be with JT's squad behind us with 240s and mortars. I was pissed that they would use the language they used, even if I knew what they meant. I didn't want that in my head or any of my guy's heads. "Bait," I thought. "Fuck that, call it something different, my guys aren't bait. And what the hell does the hideaway squad need an MG team for? We are consistently getting hit at 300 plus; the bait could use the machine guns!" Problem with all that thinking was that it was vocalized out loud with personality. "This is stupid!" I said, nodding to SSgt. Wright. He then said, "Rogers, I swear to God you are the biggest coward in the planning phase and the most feared when you're in the execution phase. You want me to church it up, 'meander' about smartly until you achieve contact; and I'm keeping the gun team with us."

I grimaced and then let out a chuckle. He was right, it made more sense to have the 240s with JT, but I was right about my boys not being referred to as 'bait' out loud. As the first few particles of sunlight broke the horizon, we were sliding off the roof down a makeshift ladder onto the top of some dried-out poppy stems, and then to the ground and preparing to move. We echeloned out of our compound in twos until the entire squad was out in the open, and then opened our dispersion to about 50 meters front to back.

As we moved through the field you could feel the eyes upon you, yet no round cracked off. You could feel the hate and death wishes, and yet nothing popped off. We made our way all the way across the field, now in the enemy's backyard, and made entry into a compound. This compound was the first one in a string of small huts that skirted the wadi system. Once the house was clear and security set in on the roof, we conducted a detailed search of the house and all outbuildings. The one occupant in the compound was an older lady of about 60 or so. They age so poorly that it's hard to tell, though. She had no teeth, tan leathery skin and ratty white hair. She had a mole on her chin and tan-colored manjams with a dark scarf wrapped around the waist. She had been put on her knees because the Marines in the initial entry found a Russian 9 mm pistol in the wall and several radios, wire and D-cell batteries. This is the bombmaker's marketplace, I thought. I went to talk to her with my interpreter. I asked about the weaponry and batteries and she said nothing; just looked at the ground and spat. I asked her where the Taliban were at currently and she smiled, shook her head and said, "The Taliban run this country better than America." Then she spat again. I shook my head and said, "Well, I'll take your word for it, but if you are wrong and I get shot at leaving here, I will kill you." She grabbed her one crutch and hobbled to the compound wall where she stood up on it watching us exfil the compound.

As my teams cycled by moving to the next compound in the string of huts, I watched her watching my guys moving, knowing she wanted to kill all of us, and would do it given the opportunity. I turned to join the last team in entering the next site when shots snapped over my head and the fight was on. The initial burst was about 15 or so rounds fired from at least a couple of different weapons. When I turned to find the old lady, she hadn't moved a muscle. She didn't move because she knew the fight was here already, and she wanted to watch us die. I raised up my M4 and rested it on the courtyard wall, finding her old leathery face in the RCO and putting the tip of the glowing red aimpoint chevron just between her eyes. She now had a two-way radio in hand communicating to enemy forces. With less than 10 pounds of pressure from my index finger, I kept my word and ended that lady's existence. I turned around and focused my attention back on the squad who now was being aided by JT and SSgt. Wright with a pair of machine gun teams. The enemy was caught up in the fires not knowing where JT was hitting them from and shut fires down. After a few small exchanges we entered a lull in the fight. In the lull, all the guys would get food, water and top-off ammo. We had a long day ahead of us and needed to stay hydrated and consuming calories for the fight.

I had men posted up on the roofs and were now coordinating how to best squeeze the enemy with SSgt. Wright. The new plan was to essentially clear the entire sector daring them to keep fighting us. "So, it was said and so it shall be, roll it up boys, we're pressing on." I struck up a Newport, took a deep pull and exhaled the smoke into the equally hot air. I told the team leaders we would be traveling and overwatching with JT's squad south of us, mirroring our movement. This became commonplace throughout our time in Marjah, especially when the battlefield was kinetic. We moved out and echeloned to the next compound, and then the next. From there we popped to the roof and covered the sector as JT and SSgt. moved to the next compound up in front of them, always mutually supporting one another's positions. As we moved through the sector it was readily obvious that these people hated us and were most certainly in the tight grips of the Taliban. The lady I shot in the contact earlier was so weird because she seemed to be orchestrating some of the fight, in a place where they practice Sharia law. She likely was tied in well with the local Taliban, either aid and support or family-related. At any rate, it struck me as extremely odd after the fact.

As we watched JT's squad move, I spotted SSgt. Wright and Herby moving along a long courtyard perimeter wall. It led into a main courtyard which had several small outbuildings in it. From my vantage point I couldn't see into the dead space behind the courtyard wall, meaning it was going to be difficult to cover them once they entered the compound. There was no time to radio this information to them, as they were in a steady jog echeloning toward the opening. I pulled out of my RCO and directed my guys to the area I was concerned about when shots erupted into the air, each burst feeling as though it sucked a bit of your oxygen right out of your chest, with the percussion. My heart fell as I knew Herby and Wright had just crossed into the open danger area of the courtyard. As the fight raged, I kept listening on the hook for someone to call for support. I rolled my guys up and made an abrupt exit heading for Wright and Herby when SSgt. broke the silence and said they were safe. They had taken contact as they moved down the wall but mitigated the threat. I notified them that I would be moving past their compound to the south for a foothold and would get up with them when I was set. They had to sort out some BDA stuff and recollect anyway.

With the MGs on the roof covering our movement, we made our way to the last house in the sector still needing attention. It was all quiet as we moved, just the sound of muffled gear and heavy-breathing Marines. Once in the last compound we popped tall to get eyes again on JT's squad and cover their movement. When the squad was set, I hit the PTT and called to JT, "2-3 this is 2-2, I'm set here." SSgt. Wright broke in, "Hey Rogers that's a wrap for the area but you know how these assholes are when we start to RTB; keep your head on a swivel and give 'em hell if they try anything." "Fair enough," I replied. That was SSgt. Wright's reply phrase for everything back then.

As they moved out of the house, they looked good, squared away, every Marine holding his respective sector, keeping enough dispersion but not too much. I was always impressed when I was able to watch the Marines do their jobs. They are amazing at what they do. I watched and scanned the sector to the north past 3rd Squad through my RCO. Nothing was stirring. The squad was split; Wright and the guns would move down south of my position to the next foothold 300 meters away, and JT and his remaining squad and ANA would take a wider route out across the fields. When they turned south in the fields, they were about 500 meters out or so. To the east behind them was another canal system with another string of dwellings skirting it. SSgt. had just said they were set in their house and movement was on JT.

As 3rd Squad moved south through the open field, I had all my M249 SAWs on the roof with Charette and Grimes. This maximized my fire support power if the need should arise. As we watched our brothers cross the field, I picked up some movement in the string of compounds behind them. It looked like someone with a mortar tube on the back of his moped. I briefly saw him, and he was gone again behind a compound. Then the outgoing mortar sounded off and we knew the time to fight was here once more and the hot chow back inside the wire was now a fantasy.

I quickly ran toward the courtyard wall to the east to use it as a gun rest while firing. The enemy ripped off about a 15- to 20-round burst from a PKM-style belt-fed weapon before the mortar could even land. They were bearing down on JT's men when the mortar exploded just outside my wall about 50 meters. I dropped to a knee as the air was sucked from the sky. Then a second mortar exploded, putting me down further. I hadn't heard the second outgoing shell and was rocked again. I couldn't hear much, and my vision was a bit blurry. I looked to the roof and said, "Fire now," and hit the moped, standing back up firing tracers at his last-known position. The squad laid down a wall of lead and I was able to move to a better vantage point. The MGs with Wright and Herby were now rocking as well. Over the radio I heard that JT had guys down in the field and was moving to cover in a small compound to address the injuries. SSgt. Wright broke in, "2-2 I need you to go assist with JT in the CCP, if needed get the CASEVAC moving along." "Roger SSgt. I'm Oscar Mike [On the Move]." I turned things over to Charette and the team leaders and told them what I was doing. JT's triage compound was a short 200 meters away. I would take a small number of ANA with me as a security element and go straight to JT's position.

When I left the compound, the fight was still raging. My guys had killed the moped mortarman, and were still exchanging rounds with pockets of enemy. SSgt. Wright and Herby were controlling MG fires from the south onto the enemy and JT was held up triaging a down man. As I sprinted through the field in a small irrigation ditch, all I could think about was getting in there and helping. I radioed JT where I would be coming from and he confirmed me in. He sent out Cole Wolbeck, one of his team leaders, to be the connecting file and get me in the right building. Wolbeck plopped down into the ditch to lead me in. He had blood all over him. "You hit?" I asked. "Nah man, this ANA guy in here is fucked though."

Inside the compound that was no bigger than a decent-sized walk-in closet was Randique, an ANA commando who just weeks earlier had pulled the pin out of his grenade because he was instructed to stand post at night for a shift that he didn't want to stand. He was most certainly more against us than with us throughout my time there. He lay crying in the floor, now begging the same Marines he intended to injure or kill over a night post, to save his life. He was hit high in the left thigh cutting his femoral artery, and high in the shoulder by the armpit. There was blood squirting out of his leg spraying blood all over the place. Both spots are very hard to successfully tourniquet off. He was called in as a priority pick-up as his life was literally hanging in the balance. JT went outside to check the area and got a yellow smoke ready to pop for the bird that was inbound. The plan was for Wolbeck and I to buddy-carry this guy in to the LZ and get him on the bird. He had the soldier's armpit area and I was at his legs. As we picked him up the blood-covered gear was so slippery that it was hard to maintain a good grip. After a short movement I set the soldier down and told Wolbeck I would get him and to cover my six with JT. I hoisted the man up into a fireman carry and began to move down the sand drive to the field. I had to cross a small irrigation ditch, the same one I moved through to get to the compound. As I approached the ditch my thought was to drop down with both feet at the same time to maintain control of the soldier I was carrying. When I dropped down the soldier groaned and his femoral gushed blood across my face into my right eye and onto my lips. Instantly I climbed up the other side where JT had just popped smoke. I continued toward the smoke with the Helo inbound 30 seconds out, dry heaving the entire way. As the bird made its final descent to the earth his rotor washes completely rolled JT and Wolbeck back several feet. The only reason I didn't get blown over was because of the man on my back. The extra weight kept us grounded as "Dustoff" sat down directly on the smoke canister. The crew helped me get Randique on the bird and I tapped his chest and turned back for the house.

Thinking back now to all the training I conducted or took part in over the years to that point, I was training for these very times, when 2Bravo at the beginning of the deployment had the squads compete for privileges such as being first to chow or the barber shop. One of the competitions was a fireman carry 50 or so meters and back. Each squad leader took off at the same time. My squad finished first. LT and SSgt. used to say competition breeds results, and I couldn't have agreed more. I learned a lot from both and contribute much of my success to the two of them while in country.

With the mission ending, more attention was clearly needed in the northern sector. We were informed that day would be upon us shortly. Something needed to be done about it before 2/9 came into zone. Our relief was said to be here soon, and I could almost see myself leaving Marjah after all.

5-Day War

The deployment was nearing the end and the relief would be on the ground in just a short time. As much as you don't want to do anything risky this close to going home, you also want to set your oncoming unit up for success. If we drew into the wire and played it safe it would put not only the oncoming unit in danger because of the freedom of movement for the enemy being restored, it would also put us as a unit in the same type of danger. To mitigate this threat and set up 2/9 for success we put into motion an op to go north in the enemy's backyard yet again and bang it out. We would take over some real estate up north, close to the northern bubble, then proceed to blow up as many of their service bridges as we could to entice them to fight and impede the freedom of movement that they had been enjoying. This operation would turn quickly into a violent assault that essentially raged on for five days.

The plan straightforward: we were to make our way north from the COP and set up a patrol base (PB) in an area chosen by SSgt. Wright. It would be my squad and JT's squad, SSgt. Wright, Herby and his two machine gun teams, and a section of mortarmen wielding 60 mm mortars. Each man was issued 10 additional sandbags to carry and fill to reinforce our posts at our PB once there. We would make our way up, set in and immediately begin to pump out patrols to destroy the bridges in question. Our guess was that it wouldn't take long to declare TIC (troops in contact) and decisively engage the enemy. We were correct.

Summer was in full swing at this point and the temps during the daytime were soaring. It was common to be around 110 or 115 degrees at sunup. Movement under full loads is difficult, to say the least, and water consumption is imperative. Everyone in the squad laced up yet again and topped off all water bladders. Each man was instructed to pack out at least three days of supply (DOS) of water and chow. We would have the ability to be reinforced if needed but we wanted to keep that to a minimum if possible. This would quite possibly be the last operation with my squad on this scale before 2/9 came in for the Relief in Place Transition of Authority (RIPTOA).

Thoughts of a big-scale offensive like this one, this close to the end of the deployment, have a tendency to do things to the psyche. As I conducted pre-combat checks and inspections prior to stepping off, I made it abundantly clear to my men that we would not be fucking around on this one. Everything we had done and accomplished to this point as a squad would mean nothing if this went badly. I told them to take no chances, call up everything suspicious and as I had said many times before, I told them it was better to be judged by 12 than carried by six. Everyone nodded in the silence and the point was clearly taken.

Following this operation up north our main element was set to be replaced by that of 2/9 which would leave the squad leaders and LTs to finish out the transition. We would fly out a week or so after the main body. I shook out the thoughts of what was to come and worried about getting my radios to the COC to get the new crypto fill. (encryption filled into the radios to give us secure communications) While I was up there, I got a hot cup of coffee and conversed with SSgt. Wright and some others around the map in the arctic air, soaking in what I could as it would be all hot and all bad the next few days.

I was personally excited about this operation because it was something that needed to be done for some time. We had always talked about going up to the northern bubble and fucking these guys up, but there was always a reason we were unable to pursue them, even when we were already engaged. I understood that there were a lot of moving parts and things that got in the way, deconflicting air and ground assets from us to the Royal Marines' AO. We always wanted to run up there and now it had come together. They were going to be pissed and brazen. When they are pissed and brazen, we get to kill more of them. Which is fun for us and good for the new unit coming into zone.

We would be stepping off under the cover of darkness and make our movement out of the bazaar and north using multiple routes. We would end up cordoning off the tentative patrol base and then moving to secure it. Once secured, posts would be immediately established, and a working party would be filling sandbags to reinforce the posts. At the same time, the first patrol would push out at sunup to demo the first of a series of bridges. EOD would roll attached and systematically we would destroy the Taliban's supply routes until they fought us.

There were several times that I worked with JT's squad throughout the course of the deployment and we always worked well together. Scotty was in this squad and that made it nice when we worked together. Scotty and I would chill in the downtime. That again goes to the brotherhood of the warrior. It's always like a family reunion after just a few days of being apart or engaged. Literally, with life hanging in the balance, you would only find out you lost someone from another squad way after the fact. We all were happy to see each other anytime we could. Getting to operate with one another was even better.

With the whole tripod intact, we stepped off under the cover of darkness to test our fate once more, or should I say to test their fate once more. Herby and guns would roll with SSgt. Wright up to the PB with JT's squad, and we would have the mortars with us and the new EOD techs in the AO. It was a relatively short movement to the area we wanted to set up in, as it was only a few clicks north of Five Points. The idea again was to set up in the backyard of the enemy and force him to fight us or watch us blow up all his supply routes.

Two additions to the squad before stepping off were the left seat to my squad from 2/9 (our relief). The key leaders from the 2/9 were on deck and the squad leader taking over my AO as well as one of his Cpl. team leaders were to be attached to my hip and welcomed to the AO. I spoke to Sgt. Soto briefly before heading out, ensuring him and the Cpl. both that we would be fighting on this operation and it would be highly kinetic. He remained cool the best he could. I told him to watch the locals and talked to him about establishing a baseline for activity.

The movement to the compound was dark and quiet, just how we wanted it to be. JT and his boys made entry into the compound we would be living out of for the next several days and we moved through to supplement and provide rooftop overwatch. Once things were secure, the squads went into action hardening the compound and filling sandbags to create a more defendable rooftop post. If we hurried, we would have some defendable positions when the sun greeted us in a couple of hours. If we had the element of surprise in the daylight hours, we felt good about the movement.

Once the rooftop posts were established and the mortars had created their firing platforms and pits, we started to generate a patrol and post roster to be adhered to for the next three to five days. We would constantly send our patrols to demo bridges and conduct contact patrols, saturating the area with our presence and daring the Taliban to come play. It would take much enticing for them to oblige.

On our first patrol out as a squad we were set to exit the PB-friendly lines to the south and ride an east-west running irrigation ditch for almost a click. Then we would move into the poppy fields and open way up in a staggered column and begin to work the area. When Wetzel made the left around the building, we took contact from the west southwest. His TL, Cpl. Charette, grabbed and pulled him back to the corner and he laughed and said we should go out the other side. We got a chuckle and moved to the north exit. From there we had enough micro terrain to the west to impede our movement from the Taliban marksman. We weren't sure how many fighters were plotting but at least one of them had fired, presumably through one of the many catholes in the mud hut walls. They were what we called the small firing ports etched out by the enemy. On some occasions we gave this medicine right back to them.

Now out and moving through the irrigation ditch as a squad reinforced, I got some chatter from Knucks on the black gear: "Yo Sergeant I got an active spotter back here. Requesting permission to hit him."

"Roger. Light him up," I said, and I halted to squad and awaited the snaps. Sgt. Soto looked at me as if to ask what the hell we were doing and I quickly filled him in on the active and passive spotters. I waited for what seemed to be a lot longer than I should have before finally hearing a nice, controlled pair rattle off to the rear of the formation. SSgt. Wright from the PB just 300 meters behind us squawked in for a SITREP.

"2-2 this is 2Bravo, is the spotter down?"

"2Bravo this is 2-2, that's an affirm."

I then called back to Knuckles through the black gear and asked *what took so damn long?* He replied that he wanted to take the shot from the sitting position, and he was getting his natural respiratory pause. I laughed and we continued with the patrol. Unbeknownst to us on patrol, that very commander walked up to our PB after being shot and sought out medical attention. Doc Hernandez patched him up and sent him to a hospital to the north. He wanted to go under his own power, so he was afforded that opportunity. We pushed the patrol up to the north and let everyone who didn't already know that we were here. JT was set to take the next patrol out and blow some bridges. I would be on react and have my boys manning the PB posts.

We continued the patrol to recon the area and felt the eyes of hate on us the entire time but didn't achieve contact with the enemy. We RTB some two hours later. We found out about the spotter upon our return to the patrol base. The ICOMM chatter Marine picked up traffic that the downed spotter was a commander. This may have been why things were so quiet for the remainder of our walkabout.

When JT was out, he was also engaged, and they banged it out for a good portion of the afternoon and into the early evening. Several 60 mm mortars were dropped for him and they had air on station a few times. By the close of night, number one of the five-day war we had already been in had multiple decisive engagements and the enemy was not overly happy with us. To be sure, day two would harbor much of the same, but as for our counts…. We were still good.

The next morning, we set out for the northern bubble once more and were moving cautiously through the poppy when the atmospherics all changed, and we knew we were about to be in a gunfight. We tightened up as a squad and I called in to SSgt. Wright my current SITREP.

"2Bravo this is 2-2, we are about to be in a TIC, how copy?"

"Roger 2-2 that's a solid copy, we are standing by with the 60s, what do you got?"

"2Bravo I have multiple MAMs actively spotting my patrol, jumping in and out of the alleyways and it looks like more MAMs moving through the east and west running tree line to the north of me."

"2Bravo be advised I'm going to begin to echelon my squad across the road and into the adjacent tree line. Stand by for contact."

"2-2 Roger, that's a solid copy on all, standing by."

You could always hear it in SSgt. Wright's voice that he would rather be beside you than calling in fires for you. I gave Charette the nod, and then he and Wetzel crossed the culvert. Charette had a full belt of 40 mm grenades in waiting and one ready in the tube. He would initiate contact with his M203 to let everyone know it was time to kill. It also had a shock and awe effect on the enemy when he did this, which always worked to our advantage.

As soon as Charette was set with point on the other side of the culvert I moved Grimes up by me. I told him to stay low and to get the SAW set up and ready to engage the whole group spotting as soon as we achieved contact. In the compound we were moving from was Knuckles with the third team reinforced by some ANA. They were on the rooftop and maintaining security on the spotters and the MAMs in the trees to the north of the spotters. The new Cpl. from 2/9 loaded a 40 mm grenade into his M203 breach and trained his eyes on the tree line. His lips were chalky white as the nerves in him were shaken.

No more than did I start my movement across the street than the entire battlespace seemingly erupted with gunfire. The positive thing was that we knew it was coming and were able to instantly have rounds moving back downrange at the enemy and we instantly achieved rounds on target. This was not enough to stifle the enemy in the trees, but we sure put the spotters in the alley down. Over the black gear I heard Herby who was observing the fight from the PB with Scotty Davis and SSgt. Wright say, "Get your boys low Rogers, Scotty's got the thumper!"

The thumper he was referring to is the Mk 34 grenade launcher. It fires 40 mm grenades from a six-shooter essentially and he had 12 rounds coming in as fast as he could deliver them. I heard enough and told the squad to only shoot what they could hit and to enjoy the show, that Scotty was wielding the thumper. Instantly the sound of the thumper's incoming grenades littered the tree line. A brief pause to reload and then the rain fell again, stifling the battle space. This brief lull gave me a minute to collect my thoughts and sort out a plan for conducting the battle damage assessment (BDA).

We postured up awaiting the counterattack and organized teams for exfil. The snaps began to pop off from the area where the spotters were moving through the alleyways, followed directly by all three SAWs opening up, two from the roof and the other from the ground, as well as multiple M203s being launched. With the fight raging once more, we banged it out, moving from our one compound into another to the north, driving the Taliban back. Soon, enough of them would die and the rest would bug out. We bounded and overwatched one another until we came to the end of the sting of compounds, ending up in a rather nice compound with good roof access and visibility. It happened by chance, as this was the last in the line to be cleared out. We would consolidate and RTB.

On the way back to the PB one of the Marines mentioned needing to stop at the cigarette shop and grab some smokes for the PB. I concurred while lighting up my own American Newport, saying, "Wetzel, push south east back to the ditch and then run that back by the shops. We will hold for a quick buy and then push on."

Everyone was already smoked and there was no telling how long we would stay; maybe another day, maybe longer. When we dropped into the irrigation ditch and started toward the bazaar area, we were called by 2Bravo on black gear.

"Rogers, prepare to defend yourself, the ICOMM Marines have chatter about a squad of Marines IVO the bazaar and are prepping to ambush."

"2Bravo that's a solid copy, we are at that bazaar now."

I scanned the sector to find nothing out of the norm, which is not saying much as we had been in contact a good portion of the day. All my key leaders in the squad had black gear on them and heard what I heard. The information was passed about the squad and everyone tightened up quick. The quick buy went well, and we eased back to the PB with no ambush.

Either the enemy just decided they weren't going to fuck with us this day, or the ICOMM chatter was referring to a completely different squad in or out of the AO. Either way we were now back under the cover of the PB posts and able to shed some of the weight. My guys got some chow and many went straight up to post to relieve JT's guys. They would then come down to eat, sleep, clean weapons and prepare for the next patrol.

Throughout the time we had been on patrol banging it out with the enemy, another group was taking shots at our rooftop post at the PB. While we were out, the other squad added more bags topside and enhanced the posts. The next fight they would be better prepared and protected. As the night fell on day two in the bubble, I ate chow and hashed out with SSgt. Wright the marching orders for the following day. SSgt. Wright would roll with us. He couldn't take not being in the fight any longer.

We would again be hitting the northern sector of the bubble and would saturate the enemy's backyard once more. The plan was to move north all the way to the 92 northing and set up shop. Charette would let me know when we arrived, as would be rolling in the rear on this movement. I had anticipated being hit from the rear toward the PB, if from anywhere. I would have a heavier squad and the help of 2Bravo throughout. I shook the thoughts of the next day out of my head and moved out to the hygiene area and scrubbed my body with a water-bottle shower and a bar of Irish Spring. I then shaved my face and brushed my teeth.

At some point during day three, JT was out of the wire engaged and the mortars were falling on the enemy. The 60s were firing now from the handheld mode led by Cpl. Wilson as JT called in his adjustments to SSgt. Wright. Wright would relay the information to the guns and the rounds were out and on the way.

They would often have the rounds set to explode right above the ground as we were being engaged primarily from tree lines that skirted the compounds and wadis.

Soon as we observed the fight to the northeast of our position, the smoke settled and the only thing you could hear were the intermittent pops from the small arms in JT's element, and the occasional burst of one of the attached 240s. As the battle space fell quiet, one lone gunman on a moped was seen exiting the fight with guns in tow. SSgt. Wright instantly called the mortar team to action as he was out of range for our small arms weapons. Herby acted as a firing stake, holding his arm straight up from his shoulder and in line with the man on the moped out on the courtyard wall. The tube strokers calculated flight time and lead, letting the round fly and inserting another one for the follow-up adjustment. We all watched in extreme anticipation, awaiting the impact.

Cpl. Wilson called out three seconds and we peered over the wall to get eyes to make quick adjustments and fire for effect. The shot was money. When the round impacted, the man was directly in the middle of the plume. It was quite shocking to see. You always dream about a direct hit like this, but it never happens like this. A handheld 60 with a Marine's arm as a firing stake, on a moped-borne moving target a few thousand meters! The shot was hands down the best/luckiest mortar shot I have ever witnessed. With the impact being "dead on," literally, we all hooped and cheered giving daps and hugs to the whole team of gunners, tackling the Corporal to the ground in admiration. No BDA was necessary. 2Bravo got on the hook with JT and informed him the guy that squirted out was neutralized and he was good to continue with his op.

The fourth day came much the same as the preceding three. However, now it was time to head to the 92 and with 2Bravo and a team of medium machine guns we planned to press them hard. The idea was to get to the 92 so we could post up and observe the area and gauge atmospherics. As said by Cpl. Charette, he mentioned the op afterwards and said, "This movement was one of the freakiest. We knew they were around us, amongst us even, but we did not get engaged."

We continued to observe for about 45 minutes and the atmospherics were the same as they had been thus far. Not good. The next movement would be to push further east maintaining the 92 northing and force them to fight, as we continued to travel and overwatch utilizing every building in the area with decent roof access. Our first roof was perfect with a staircase and a center room that was dead center of the compound and had great visibility to all directions. We had used this building a few times so far and it was working out well.

We rolled it up after a while and began to push to the east yet again. Moving into the next compound we were greeted by a small child and her father. They had been making pita bread on the bottom of a heated-up metal bowl. The bowl was about the size of a big cereal bowl with a small fire underneath. I had never seen anything like it. She must have been four or five years old, and she would knead the dough and throw it on the back of the small bowl. All spread out and forming, with bare hands, she would grab the dough and flip it like a pizza, landing the uncooked dough on the bowl to finish. She looked at the Marines as they walked in gesturing that they should have some bread.

After the first Marine accepted the bread and smiled as he bit into it and thanking her, she hurried back to the bowl and put out one for each man, cooking them in mere seconds, then flipping them like you would a frisbee to each of the guys. It was hot and it was delicious. Made me think again back to Americans and how privileged our children are to be born in America versus anywhere else. After a short snack from a caring family, we pushed on to hunt the enemy, leaving the young girl and her father to be in relative peace.

After a one-click movement through a poppy field we ended up in a rather nice compound for the area and were again posted up, watching for the enemy. This building had a ton of plants and vines. It was a nice compound and easily defendable. The air came alive as the shots rang out to the north. Instantly 2Bravo, Charette, the guns and I exited to maneuver under the cover of the rooftop posts manned by Knuckles and company. There was a small irrigation ditch running east and west that was right off the south courtyard wall. We needed to move to the west, back toward the patrol base, as they were staying to the north of us, and there wasn't any great cover to the east.

As the fire grew more and more intense, I departed Charette and SSgt. making my way back into the firm base. I popped to the roof to get better situational awareness on the enemy locations. I saw multiple muzzle flashes from the tree line to the north and removed the M67 shoulder-fired LAW off my own back, this time to prep for a shot. I was carrying the LAW on my back as Charette wasn't about to carry it and have me shoot it again. He was overly bitter the past two times that had happened. I made the shot as the sun was fading in the evening sky and the tree line fell momentarily silent.

With dusk upon us the TLs got everyone to attach their night vision devices. We would be fighting in the dark on the way back if these assholes wouldn't bug out. In a lull we decided to make the move out to the south and echelon in pairs through an irrigation ditch back to the east, to the original house we had been in just a few hours prior. Charette's team was almost to the next piece of cover when the Taliban marksman opened once more.

With half of the squad in the east-west running ditch I called out to the boys by me that we would be peeling. I radioed it across black gear to the key leaders and we started to peel as a squad reinforced, each man digging to get to the end and slapping the next man in the peel as he ran by. The peel was absolutely amazing. The squad was firing on all cylinders and the movement was sexy as hell, laying down fire through the peel for more than 200 meters. Once back to the original observation building, we were able to pop the MG to the roof and lay it on the enemy hard. So hard, in fact, that the sear in the MG broke, creating a runaway gun momentarily and then deadlining one of the two MGs we had with us. A runaway gun is what we call it when the machine gun continues to fire when the trigger is released. This happens for a few different reasons, but this day the sear notch had busted.

I had been notified from every team leader that they were getting very low on ammunition and that the MGs were red as well. SSgt. took over calling in to the PB to get Palmer up from Five Points with some more rounds just in case we needed them. He would be meeting us at the OP if things worked out well in this gunfight.

Thankfully, the remaining Taliban fighters bugged out and we were able to safely RTB with no injuries to the squad or attachments. When we came in to the PB we saw Palmer's squad making its way to us with the resupply. It would no longer be necessary as we had gotten word we would be leaving in the morning. That was an awesome feeling, knowing that it was only a short amount of time left until we had to go back in order to rip out with 2/9's main element. After the main body was out of zone I could for the first time relax and worry only about myself. Even if everything went to shit, I would know that all my guys were out of zone and to safety.

Transition of Authority

Late that evening we broke down all of the posts on the roof and gathered all of our gear and comfort items in preparation to move back to Five Points early in the morning hours. Everyone had a bit of a buzz about them knowing that they had just finished the last patrol and combat operations, God willing. Many of us felt excited to get back, and many of us were just for the first time of the deployment coming to grips with the fact that we would be making it out of this place not only alive but proven in the ultimate arena.

The walk back to the COP was uneventful and passed like a blur. When we returned, all gear was cleaned and staged to be flown out of zone. I would be remaining back with the key leaders to conduct the final portion of the turnover of the battle space to the Marines of Victor 2/9. Charette would lead the squad through this phase, until we reunited a few days later on Camp Dwyer.

I would remain with the other squad leaders and LT. A select number of other officers and staff remained from the company and from the other platoons who were likewise doing the same things. We conducted two or three patrols with the new squad taking over and helped them through the transition phase in any way that we could. I didn't know it then, but this place and the hard-working men of 2/9 would meet very stiff opposition after we left, and the Medal of Honor actions of Kyle Carpenter would take place.

On the final few patrols, it would be myself and LT from Kilo 3/6, and then Sgt. Soto's entire element. It was not fun to me working with Marines other than my own. I didn't like how things ran in Soto's squad, but it worked for them. I realize now that it didn't matter who took over, they wouldn't compare to my squad in my eyes.

After the left seat patrols were out of the way, it was time to get the hell back home. First stop Dwyer. LT and I had talked about getting back in time to hit up the main chow hall. They had things like chili cheese burritos and salad bars and soda. We were like kids talking about our favorite fat-boy snacks. The word was that we would be leaving Marjah in a CH46 and it would go at 0400 hours under the cover of darkness. At 0400 the bird was delayed for some reason and they didn't get to the COP until 0900 in the broad daylight. Everything was so fast after that. We shuffled onto the bird knowing that there was a good possibility it would take some sort of fire as we pulled out of there.

With all the leadership loaded up the bird started to lift off. I was sitting directly across from Captain Biggers on the bird and we locked eyes, both with a bit of fear about the speed in which we weren't going. The pilot's slow take-off had everyone shaken and then in a moment we were gone, high up in the sky, away from the filth and the dander below. I was excited to see my guys and get a hot shower, but I fully intended on running to the chow hall for some good food as soon as we touched down. LT and I talked about it all night the night prior. It was about to go down.

As we flew across the sky it became real to me that we would make it home. This wasn't something I had prepared for, but I was ready to be there. As the bird touched down at Dwyer the landscape had changed a good bit. They now had a full runway for big C-130s and planes of that class. It was really built up from the last time we were there. The chow hall was a short run and we were now in a hurry to make it before it shut down for the evening. LT and I rushed and got into the line just in time, though we were all the way at the back.

In front of us in the line were two Marines, one black, one white, and both were high-ranking enlisted men. The had freshly starched desert digital utilities on and smelled of Curve cologne for men. They had clean everything. Clean haircuts, clean shaves, clean boots and trousers that were bloused high enough over their boots to see their clean black socks. I didn't notice them until the one turned around in line and told me that I stunk and needed to get a shower and some new cammies on before I came back in the chow hall.

My emotions came out as I gripped my M4 and started to give this man a piece of my mind, when LT stepped in to have a more officer-to-enlisted conversation and clear things right up for him. It didn't seem to be a big problem after the conversation ended. I will say that it has stuck out to me this far afterwards, and it's people like that man who lose all bearing on what we are doing in these countries. Then they spoil the fight for the lot of us. Don't be that guy.

Following the best meal ever, I was shown to the berthing and met up with the squad. They were in a mean game of spades when I walked in and saw everyone. We were assigned a large GP tent that held all three squads. I dropped my shit on an unclaimed rack and breathed deep. Grimes popped down on me and said, "Yo Sergeant we going to make it outta here?"

To which I replied, "You want the truth or the lie, fat boy?"

Everyone laughed hard and continued their games, as this was my ongoing response through the whole deployment. I took this time to take a shower and square away my gear. We would be palletizing gear for the move and flying from Dwyer back to Manama Air base from where we first came, then a long flight to Germany and finally home to Cherry Point, NC.

During the layover in Germany the CO cleared everyone to drink two beers per. He said we earned it and to enjoy them. Herby and I gathered our beers and challenged the CO and the Company First Sergeant to a game of spades. We had heard that they were good and that they were talking shit on us. They accepted the challenge and the cards were dealt. I don't know how many times we beat them on the layover, but I know that the company was told they could get more beer until we were beat...which didn't happen soon. The entire company had warmed up their blood for the final trip to the states and would be getting mighty sleepy. I was notified by the LT upon boarding that I would be riding up in the first-class section with him as they had some extra seats available. First and last time I have ever flown first-class; it was awesome.

Once home we made our way from Cherry Point, NC, to Camp Lejeune, where we would open the armory and turn in all weapons and serialized gear. This was a smooth process, and so smooth that most of the guys had time to run to the bricks and spruce up. We also had several dozen roses waiting for us at the armory that were to be given to the wives and mothers on the march up to the parade deck.

Each platoon was then called to attention and reported the company in to First Sergeant Petrakas. With the numbers up we were faced and marched in company formation to the parade field, where the homecoming was commencing with our families. About halfway through the movement the entire company got a surprise as the retirement canon went off up by the parade deck where our families were waiting. The entire company swerved to the right, damn near hitting the deck, then popped back tall and resumed the march. We all laughed slightly and then found our bearing once more. The company was halted and then dismissed to our families. We laughed and shared beers right in the parking lot. I spoke to many parents and friends.

Ten years have passed since I left Marjah and not a day goes by that my thoughts are not with the men of Kilo Company Victor 3/6, and the Marines who never left that place. After 10 years of trying to get this book right, I give it to you and the world as an account of what we did in a time that was filled with hate. I miss you all, I love you all, and I thank you all from the bottom of my heart.

ACKNOWLEDGMENTS

From the start it is important to say that it would be impossible to list all the people in my life that have made a profound impact on me and the ultimate path I chose in life that has led to the publication of this memoir.

First to my wife, who is the most loyal and patient soul I have ever met. I love you and cannot thank you enough for the support and the life you have helped me to lead. Without you I would be lost. During the writing of this book, you were by my side supporting me and driving me to continue even when life was beating me down. For that I am forever grateful.

To my children Kinley, Brantley and Kenady Jane, I love you more than words can ever describe, and I hope that you can forgive the amount of time spent away from you in completion of this book. Your existence in it of itself has changed me in ways you will not soon understand. Daddy loves you.

To my father John Rogers, thank you for giving me the foundational tools to be a good man. You are one of the best men that I know and have been my best friend and confidant through the trials and tribulations of life. I love you and thank you for everything you have ever done for me. In my estimation you are what encapsulates the man's man and a great father. From hunting and fishing trips as a young child to the post-war talks about not throwing my life away on alcohol, you have been my inspiration and motivational backer for much of the way. I love you.

To my beautiful mother Tracy Traugh, words could never describe the love that I have for you. You have helped build me into the person that I am today and gave me the foundational tools to lead a successful life. Thank you for always being there and offering any support that was asked for or needed. I am forever grateful for you.

To my brother John, you have always been someone that I looked up to and are still that more and more every day. You have really helped shape the man that I am and continue to do so with late night intellectual talks about life, politics, war, and literature.

You have deeply contributed in the finished copy of this book and I am forever grateful. In my estimation you are among the most influential and admirable people in my life. I love you.

To my brother Lucas, you and I share the bond of service and have had several nights of talk and tears of our days at war. You have always made time and arranged your life in black and white and I love that about you. You undoubtably have contributed to me as a man and continue to do so. You too are one of the most influential and admirable people in my life. I love you.

To my brother Tyler, many people before now would not have known the number of times that you have saved me from chaos and self-destruction. You have answered calls and walked me through difficult times in my life more than anyone else. You have always picked up the phone and regardless of the situation made time for my mental health and personal wellbeing. You have always been intellectual in you approaches and I am forever grateful for that. You are among the best people that I know, and one of the most positive. You are one of the most influential and admirable people in my life and made me better because of it. I love you.

To Gordon (LT) Emmanuel, Sir, in my life there are few men who derive more respect from me. You are one of the best men that I know, and it was a pleasure to fight in combat with you. It has also been more than a decade that I have been able to depend on you for advice and guidance. You helped pull me from the depths of hell as my life was falling apart and showed me how to become whole again. You have helped me with anything I have asked you for. For that I am forever grateful. The Marine Corps need more Gordan Emmanuels in the ranks.

To Joe Wright, you are one of the best I have seen in combat. You showed me from minute 1 in the flooded poppy fields of north Marjah how to regain control of the chaos and how to be smooth and clear-minded under fire. You are the true Marines' Marine. I will never forget the times we shared in that place and cannot thank you enough for the lessons you taught me along the way.

To "The Squad." You are the best men I have ever had the pleasure of serving with, and I would go to hell and back with you again. The honor and courage you men showed at such young ages, running into to the fire (literally) to deal out American resolve to the oppressive Taliban regime and unfortunate foreign fighters who joined them was second to none. America has always been the light for all to emulate because men like you sacrificed everything for something greater than themselves. There nothing more honorable as far as I am concerned. Until Valhalla boys!

To Matt Charette, Brother there are not words to show you the appreciation I have for you. In Marjah we started talking about this book together, taking notes, and recapping significant events for the journal after the fact. Your courage under fire is admirable to say the least and your friendship to me has been the same. You are a man, Matt, plain and simple. You should know that without your help over the past 10-plus years this book in its finished form would never have been possible. For you I am eternally grateful.

To the men of 2nd Platoon and Kilo Company, thank you for all that you did in a time when the country called on you. You are all true warriors and are some of the best war fighters I have had the pleasure of serving with. It was an honor and a privilege. Thank you!

To my editor Debbie Burke, thank you so much for all that you have done to bring this dream to fruition. You have been amazingly easy to work with and more than informative and helpful in the whole process. Thank you for being patient with me and for you amazing work. You really brought the book to completion. For that I am forever thankful.

To my graphic designer Donna Lynn, thank you for your patience and hard work. You were able to design my covers in the exact way that I envisioned them. The process was professional, and the product came out perfect. Thank you for helping this dream become a reality.

To C.J. Chivers and Tyler Hicks who were combat photographers and New York Times reporters on the ground in

Marjah with us, thank you for all you have done. From the time in Afghanistan until now you have documented combat with cameras and words for the American people to understand better, and it is necessary. You two were smooth operators under fire and possess courage that is rarely observed by most. Thank you for connecting me with photos for the book and for everything you have done for me.

To Jordan B. Peterson, from whom I have learned so much: you, sir, are a positive light in a dark time, and your messages resonate with me in a deep way. Your self-authoring program and you hours of lectures have positively influenced my life and writing. For that I am thankful.

To Jocko Willink, I have watched hours of lectures and book reviews from you. Thank you for what you do every day. You motivate millions of people with your attitude and "take" on life. Getting after it! You have positively influenced my life and my writing in a major way, for that I am forever thankful.

ABOUT THE AUTHOR

Ryan N. Rogers is a retired United States Marine, National Security professional, writer, and family man. After retiring in 2014 Ryan went to school and earned a BA in Homeland Security with a minor in Intelligence, ultimately writing along the way and falling in love with philosophy.

Made in the USA
Coppell, TX
26 April 2021

54559514R00118